Discovering
GOD'S
Counsel

More Books in the Series:

Discovering God's Sufficiency
Going beyond ourselves and experiencing the supernatural
Pastoral Health Care — Part One

Discovering God's Love
Confirming God's love through the evidence of historical facts
Pastoral Health Care — Part Two

Discovering God's Kingdom
Finding a way to understand ourselves in a complex world
Pastoral Health Care – Part Four

Discovering God's Heart
Feeling God's heart pulse is our daily challenge
Pastoral Health Care — Part Five

"I have ALS which means that my life is being taken away from me. Don't ask me how I am doing. Every day brings new challenges but I am learning to live each moment with God's presence. I am comforted knowing that the Holy Spirit is traveling each step with me. I ask for his filling every day and even every hour. I am assured of my future with Jesus. As I meditate on his Word, he provides me with his perspective on life — death and all the stuff in between. I will reach my destiny with my team supporters."

— *Cindy Smith*

"I am 100 years old and have all the special physical needs that people my age experience. The spiritual Biblical mediation method works for me. It has strengthened my faith. As I recite the promises, they become a part of my thinking process. My fellowship with God provides natural growth for me both internally and externally. I am thankful that I live with His presence."

— *William Mulder*

"I have grown up with seizures. I know what it is like to lose consciousness. I know my illness is a brain disorder that requires prescribed medicines regularly. Adjusting to the various dosages is a pain. I hate the side effects that I live with. I am enabled through the guidance of the Bible. It keeps reminding me of 'His' nearness. I am thankful for the support I have. I miss my former life and its activities. My prayer is always "keep me close to you, God, and my family!" Discovering God's Sufficiency has challenged me to be close to Jesus Christ."

— *George Odiorne*

"My Life has always looked a little different. I was born with spina bifida and fluid on my brain. I have to live with many side effects like sore back, loss of balance, terrible headaches and short term memory. I have been able to manage every day remembering that God has a purpose for my life. I have been blessed with a family that I need to be here for. Every day brings new challenges that have turned my spirit toward Scripture. To my amazement, God has promised to help me. I can't count the times that I have felt His presence. I know that God has a plan for me and he will accomplish it according to his will."

— *Judy Sharp*

"I have had MS for several years. At the present time, I have been experiencing intense nerve pain. My relationship with Christ has helped me make the adjustments that are needed to survive. I am comforted to know that I will not be stretched beyond my ability to bear. I have confidence that God's will will be accomplished in my life. I have my destiny in heaven where I will experience perfection. I know abiding in Christ is the key."

— *Chuck Boomgard*

"I live with Multiple Sclerosis which is a neurological disease that affects every part of my body. I never know from one day to the next how my body is going to be. I have more MS days than functional days. While losing my worldly independence, I have gained a powerful relationship with my God by choosing to depend upon him. My trust in God empowers me to face every day with joy."

— *Susan Clark Denny*

John's books give us hope and light. He reminds us that through Jesus we are never alone. I have certainly needed that reminder in my life and in my practice. In holding a patient's hand, and helping them through a condition or disease, reminding them that they are never alone has become the greatest gift of health care.

— *Linda M. Kunce, D.C.*

As a Christian who made a commitment to follow Christ as a teen, I have had my share of struggles. In using the book, "Discovering God's Love" it was good to read that Jesus knows what its like to live in a human body. I have received Jesus and His forgiveness, but as the book suggests, I also have power from the Holy Spirit. I should lean on Jesus. Perhaps I can be more secure in meeting the challenges of life. His book encouraged me to gain courage through prayer. The author's honesty is very special to read in this book as he reflects on his own life and struggles. I like his explanation that "the soul is where the emotions are and the mind is where the thinking takes place."

It was good for me to read that God works through weakness, and learn that the author found God with him in the middle of his struggles. My interest was peaked by the questions in Chapter 10. The answers in the book really show why we should follow Jesus. As to love, the book states that God's love is freely given and we show love by touch, words, time and excitement. Quoting Pastor Gillette, I appreciated that he sees life involved in many things, including love. God sees us as His glorious inheritance. Wonderful. Praise God!

—*Arvid W. Vandyke, Ed.D.*

True, illustrative, practical stories are like windows that unlock Bible truths and promises.

Along with masterfully orchestrated short stories should come the truth that God's Word and love has been experienced by His servants as they partner with Him in the work of rebuilding the Kingdom.

Dr. Gillette has done just that in this second book of four relating to life's essential and persistent questions posed to ministers. A gifted teacher, Dr. Gillette lives an ordinary life abiding in Christ and being an obedient servant of the Lord. As he sees God working in his life, and in the lives of those to whom he ministers, his faith is refreshed and he is encouraged to press on through life's uncertainties.

One day, I was "pressing" John for more stories of how he has experienced or seen God's love demonstrated in his own life, and in the lives of his congregants and students. He said to me, "Dr. Mulonge, in pastoring and teaching there are many days, some filled with joy and others marked with pain, that's just life." Thank God for the "all the days" that teach the mighty works, the power and matchless love of God.

Only a lifetime dedicated to nurturing, ministering, teaching, and keen insight through the power of the Holy Spirit, can produce such poignant stories that teach and challenge. Dr. Gillette has done exactly this once again.

—*Mulonge M. Kalumbula, Ph.D.*

I believe in God's sovereignty and compassion. I am learning to let go of self and to hold onto someone that can do whatever he pleases. Sometimes life is cruel, sometimes it is full of suffering, physically and psychological. A spiritual solution to meet difficult trials has become my goal. God's word carries with it no uncertainties. I want it to saturate my mind and heart.

The *Pastoral Health Care* series was created through unexpected heart disease (open heart surgery), cancer (medication and surgery), a stroke and major head injury after a car accident that also resulted in the death of my wife. I am writing this because it is helping me to develop an adequate level to supernatural, psychological and physiological adjustments. It may help you as well. It has brought me security.

—*John F. Gillette, D.Min.*

PASTORAL
HEALTH
CARE
PART 3

Discovering GOD'S *Counsel*

Applying His Spiritual Solution

To Meet Difficult Trials

JOHN F. GILLETTE
WITH JOY E. GILLETTE
Author of Discovering God's Favor

Chapbook Press
Schuler Books
2660 28th Street SE
Grand Rapids MI 49512

www.schulerbooks.com/chapbook-press

Discovering God's Counsel: Applying his spiritual solution to meet difficult trials

Copyright ©2016 — John F. Gillette. All rights reserved. Published 2016. Printed at Schuler Books, Chapbook Press, Grand Rapids, Michigan, in the United States of America.

First Edition 2016

Excerpts taken from Discovering God's Presence: A Pastoral Health Care Devotional, © 2015 by Dr. John F. Gillette, D.Min.

Distribution contact:at jjgillette@comcast.net.

ISBN 13: 9781943359509

Library of Congress Control Number: 2016958689

Cover photo: Greg Rakozy/Unsplash
Cover Design: Frank Gutbrod Graphic Design

Printed in the United States of America

The Pastoral Health Care Discovery Series was produced to help during difficult trials in life. It was developed through five volumes.

Adjustments are shared through God's sufficiency. It provides a basic spiritual solution strategy. We have to affirm, accept and adjust to God's plan of action. His superiority, sovereignty and sufficiency will bring victory.

Empowerment is given through God's love. The receiving of his Son Jesus Christ provides power. Historical facts declare the truth.

Enablement is given through God's counsel. Instruction, illumination and application provides the growing process in grace.

Encouragement is given through the awareness of God's kingdom. Learning to accept God's perspective is necessary. The Holy Spirit will travel with us in the present and the future.

Contentment is given through God's heart. The meditation model is the method to follow.

It is with great affection that I dedicate this book series to my wife, Joy, who radiates God's grace. We wrote this Pastoral Health Care Series together.

Applying God's spiritual solutions to meet us in difficult trials has become even more practical in my life with the recent death of my dear wife, Joy. This book has been reproduced in her memory. While the content is the same, my dedication has become more personal than ever before. The separation is painful but as I gather my suffering and feelings of incompleteness, I will succeed with God's peace and presence. The guidelines of this book have brought blessing to our life together. We have pursued them with great persistence. I am assured that she is in God's presence, rejoicing and at peace. I will be with her to experience God's eternal presence someday as well.

". . . blessed are they who put their trust in Him."
Psalm 2:12

This book is dedicated to my grand children Cameron, Analise, Elaina, Aliya, Isaiah and Jocelyn.

Table of Contents

Introduction *01*

FOUNDATIONAL SECTION

Chapter 1
What is my focus during dark days? *05*

Chapter 2
In whom should I believe? *08*

Chapter 3
Where do I find real love? *13*

Chapter 4
How do I maximize my faith? *17*

Chapter 5
Where does my security lie? *22*

Personal Response *24*

RELATIONAL SECTION

Chapter 6
What about God's promises? *25*

Chapter 7

Who will help me practice the promises? *34*

Chapter 8

What is the preparation in accepting the promises? *41*

Chapter 9

What enables me to experience the promises? *45*

Chapter 10

What unlocks the promises for me? *50*

Chapter 11

Do I have pure motives in regard to the promises? *56*

Chapter 12

Do the promises bring security? *59*

Personal Response *64*

INSTRUCTIONAL SECTION

Chapter 13

What makes me think that the Bible is dependable? *65*

Chapter 14

Do I have God's mindset during trials? *72*

Chapter 15

How do I saturate my thoughts with God's? *80*

Chapter 16
How do I apply God's instruction to my daily activities? *87*

Chapter 17
How do I handle the impossible situations? *96*

Chapter 18
What do I do with doubts? *100*

Chapter 19
Why be depressed? *103*

Chapter 20
What about the fear of death? *111*

Chapter 21
How can I be secure during trials? *118*

Personal Response *121*

SPIRITUAL SECTION

Chapter 22
Why should I glorify God? *122*

Chapter 23
How can I live for the glory of God? *126*

Chapter 24
What are some hindrances to living for the glory of God? *128*

Chapter 25

What priorities should I pursue to glorify God? *133*

Personal Response *136*

Sources *137*

Acknowledgements *140*

Introduction

"Discovering God's Counsel" is a spiritual solution to meet difficult trials. It has been developed through conversations that caused questions which needed answers. It has brought Biblical transformation in my own life and in the lives of others. It is discipleship at its core and is a good starting point for instruction and advice. It has and will provide solid results when applied.

Life is a process of developing an adequate level of spiritual, psychological and physiological adjustments. Each day I have experiences which may threaten my well-being in each of these areas. The pen and pain provide knowledge and confidence in God's sufficiency.

I have been blessed with a deep spiritual desire and have been given reliable resources to push me forward. Some people have a problem with the lack of interest in what I am writing about. Some people will diligently search for an answer and are perplexed with all the hindrances of the day. Some people are led down the wrong path by religious fanatics. Some people are just plain blind to the truth.

I have been blessed to have parents who have been led in the belief that Jesus Christ is Savior and Lord. They have pursued every means to instruct me in "the way truth and life" (John 14:6). My heroes would become preachers, evangelists and missionaries. Today I listen to sermons by my heroes and I can remember their faces and platform deportment.

I have been blessed to rely upon a belief system that is in a personal relationship with God through his Son and the guidance of the Holy Spirit. Biblical authority has not been doubted because when I mix the word with faith, it works. This absolute truth has become a solid rock for me. I have studied it, taught it, tested it and I have looked at the haters of the truth, the ignorant of the truth, the scholars and also believers that have a problem with it at difficult times of life.

I have been blessed to be secure in my doctrinal belief in Jesus Christ. It has been sound from the beginning. What I believed in my childhood, I believe now in my senior years. It has become steadfast in my life because I have grown in his grace. I know a lot of people that are not secure. I think they have to let go of self. The traits of self — me, myself and I — are getting in the way.

I have been blessed to live with the inner urge to follow Jesus. The Holy Spirit indwells me. He is my witness that God the Father has chosen me, God the Son has purchased me and the Holy Spirit has sealed me. The more I pursue him, I realize that he is pursuing me. The "holy urge" is always prompting me as I allow the Holy Scriptures to penetrate my being.

I have been blessed with his benefits. Christianity is practical. It gives me a life that is fruitful, abundant and overflowing. Even during unrest, worry, confusion and confrontation, God makes his presence felt. I know he is near because I am living in the moment with him. Accept the challenge and get in to every moment with him. God's greatness, goodness and graciousness will become a part of your life.

1

What is My Focus During Dark Days?

This is my story. An unexpected direction in my life was forced upon me. The decision was made for me even though I consented and signed the medical legal agreements. Heart disease and cancer are my unwelcomed enemies. I am sure many others have had equal challenges or trials way beyond mine. God is my strength and power and he makes my way perfect (2 Samuel 22:33). He has my attention right now and he will help me deal with whatever things are present and will come up later (Matthew 6:34).

As you read this testimony, you will travel with me on a journey that will discover how "God is my refuge and strength, a very present help in trouble" (Psalm 46:1). He is my refuge, "The Lord is my strength and my shield, my heart trusted in him and I am helped" (Psalm 28:7). He is my protection and guaranteed refuge. I do not have to look at all the alternatives. He has become my first resource. The preparation for the attack of the enemy has been established. Through God's grace, my will, mind and body were ready. I have peace in him. He is my strength. "The steadfast love of the Lord never ceases, his mercies never come to an end, they are new every morning, great is your faithfulness" (Lamentations 3:22). I have experienced his faithfulness. Every day has brought new challenges and uncertainties, but every morning I have obtained strength to carry me through the day. I have endurance in his strength. The process to recovery has been established.

God is not only my refuge and strength but "present help in trouble." My trouble refers to my diseases but it could refer to any trial. The enemy wants me to be defeated but God has enabled me to be victorious. I love these words of encouragement and power, "the Lord is with me as a mighty awesome one" (Jeremiah 20:11). I am learning to "gaze upon Jesus" each moment. The promise of his counsel has brought deliverance. "The Lord is my rock, my fortress, my deliverer, my Lord, my strength in whom I trust" (Psalm 18:2).

2

In Whom Should I Believe?

Jesus said, "All that the Father giveth me shall come to me." This refers to God's sovereignty in my salvation (Romans 8:29, 30). He continues in saying "and him that cometh to me" (Ephesians 1:3-6). This is my responsibility to respond. Then he ends the invitation with a guarantee "I will in no wise cast out."

The process begins with belief. "Everyone who sees the Son and believes in him" (6:40). God works through faith and faith is provided as a gift (Romans 12:3; Ephesians 2:8, 9). Listen to what Jesus has to say — don't murmur or become hardened in the heart. Keep a clear perspective and mindset. My heart was opened through his Word which actually penetrated my mind, will and emotion.

Believing involves faith (II Peter 1:1). When I believed in Jesus (John 1:12), I received the gift of faith (Ephesians 2:8, 9). Faith is the ability to choose to fellowship with God, to obey him, to love him and to acknowledge him in all areas of life through complete submission and aggressive trust.

Through faith I have been forgiven (Acts 26:18). I have a living relationship with God (Romans 1:17). I have been justified (Romans 5:1). I have a life indwelt by God (Galatians 2:20).

Faith is personal and is based on the character of the one I believe (Romans 4:17-21). It is not based on emotion or circumstances. It accepts the promises of God as true and interprets them on the basis of the attributes of God. My personal salvation was a response to God and is based on who he is (Matthew 9:28, 29; John 1:2). It was easy for me to trust Jesus because he is God. The miracles and his claims have brought me into his family. He said, "I am the bread of life." Jesus is able to give life and sustain it. My hunger and thirst has been fully satisfied through him. My relationship with God includes trust, intimacy, obedience and love. Without Jesus, life is only an existence. I had to receive or reject his invitation.

Jesus said, "I am the light." As each year in my life slips by, I see more darkness and sin around me. In this world of depression, I have discovered that Jesus shines as the light. Jesus is the very light of God that has come among his creation. Jesus is the guide and the means to understanding life and direction.

He said, "I am the door." Jesus is the entrance into God's family. Through him I have access to a life that God wants me to have. On one hand, he offers safety and on the other security. I am thankful that I have gone through that door and have experienced new life and vitality

He said, "I am the Good Shepherd." Jesus gave his life for me on my behalf and for my benefit. He is a gracious shepherd who provides for everything I need. He is efficient, skillful and kind. He loves me and cares for me. He is aware of my necessities before I am.

His quality of care is beyond compare. He is indeed a good shepherd, "the Lord is my shepherd, I shall not want" (Psalm 23). He said, "I am the resurrection." Jesus not only takes care of my temporal earthly needs but more importantly, he provides eternal life. I think the bottom line to all he says and the basis for absolute truth is the resurrection. I have placed my trust on that truth. I have been set free and there is no more frustration or futile living.

He said, "I am the way." He says come and I will take you. You cannot miss the way because I am the way. He is not only giving advice, direction and counsel. He takes me by the hand and leads me personally (Psalm 27:11).

He said, "I am the truth." I have confidence because moral perfection finds its realization in him. He is the final key to life. He speaks with final authority in words adapted to human understanding (Psalm 86:11).

He said, "I am the life." The way is the means of reaching the Father. The trust defined the righteous standards of the way. The life originated with God and lifts me out of my sin to him. "In him was life and the life was the light of man" (1:4). Christianity is the impartation of a divine vitality. "I am indwelt by the Spirit of God" (Psalm 16:11).

He said, "I am the true vine." He is real and genuine. Jesus is the source of the heavenly life. He is the only solid foundation to build upon. It is a 'must' to abide in him. This means unbroken connection is maintained. It is a constant active relationship with Jesus. "By their fruits you shall know them" (Matthew 7:16). I believe in the death and resurrection of Jesus Christ for my sin and justification with God. God's counsel involves belief.

3

Where Do I Find Real Love?

I have discovered authentic love. I hope you will be able to allow this phrase to sink deeply into your heart . . . God is love. The concept of love has been used in many different ways. It has been abused and misused. Love has to be anchored in God. Through my open heart surgery and the side effects, I have experienced God's love and my deepest desire has been fulfilled.

The knowledge of his love has fulfilled my desire through his purpose of love. I have learned that God's love always coincides with his will (Ephesians 1:4-6). His desire is to be glorified. God didn't become love after he made the world and mankind. His love is eternal. God was love before there was man or anything else. God has everything he needs. This is hard to understand with my own reasoning but keep in mind that I am writing about an infinite God. He is perfect in every way. In my deepest spiritual, psychological and physical need, I could sense his love for me. I entered into this journey with one prayer — please glorify yourself and let your will be done. Whatever happens, I am in your loving hands. I am under the umbrella of your love.

The knowledge of his love has fulfilled my desire through his manifestation of love. This is found in Christ's provision for my salvation (Romans 5:1-5, 8). God defines love through the sacrifice of his son on the cross. God's love for mankind came to earth through the death of his son. When I was lying on that table in the hospital, Jesus was looking out for me. He guided the surgeon's hands into my heart.

The knowledge of his love has fulfilled my desire through his selfless demonstration of love. Godly love "does not seek its own" (I Corinthians 13:5), but rather that which is beneficial to another. He always has my interest in mind, what is best for me, what will bring the most glory to him and what will reach to others the most. I am anxious to watch him work.

God's love is unconditional. I do not deserve it. I have not done anything to merit it. I cannot earn it but he has given it anyway. When I came out of surgery, I was in awe of his gentle hands that saved my spiritual and physical heart. He knew that my heart belonged to him. He knew the glory he would receive through the mending of that diseased heart. He knew his son's death gave that heart life. He knows even now what he wants to do with it. All I have to do is bow before him in praise and thanksgiving. In commitment and dedication, I will continue to serve and live for eternity. It is safe to say no one else has ever loved me like that. He put his life on the line for me so I might live not only here on earth but for eternity forever with him.

The knowledge of his love has fulfilled my desire through his determination to care for me (Romans 8:31, 32). Just think of it — if God is for me, who can be against me? God is not only interested in getting me to heaven, but he cares for my comprehensive well-being. I will have trials. In saying this, I am not saying that God has deserted me. As a matter of fact, I will experience overwhelming victory. God started me off with "no condemnation" and keeps me with "no separation" (Romans 8:39). The knowledge of his love has fulfilled my desire to experience his love. When I live for his glory (which is what he loves) and when I am really consumed with living for God's glory, I will experience his love. Lord, I don't know why I am going through this situation and I don't understand it, but I am sure glad to know you love me. How can I glorify you right now? Prevailing prayer keeps me connected to Jesus. My conscientious spirit of communion fused by the Holy Spirit provides the way.

4

How Do I Maximize My Faith?

I have been redeemed for something far beyond myself, my time, my space and my history. I am a citizen of another world. "I must view clearly this world, embrace the world beyond and live by the power of the resurrected world within."

The world I live in is the domain of my adversary. I will experience the effects of this place. Through my recent experiences, heaven has become more real and relevant. Heaven is not a spiritual fantasy land. It must be my transforming point of reference. The threat of death is simply the door to all that is better. The resurrection of Christ and his post-resurrection appearances have given a sense of the reality of the world to come. I am empowered and energized with this truth. I am a child of Christ's kingdom. This took place when I believed in him and committed my life to him. The king reigns in my life. I am learning that my life does not belong to me. I am not to manage it through my own passions, pride or personal prompting. This world does not offer safety, security or satisfaction. All things in life have to be seen in light of the kingdom to come. I have to be surrendered to the king that lives within me. I have to practice obedience to his Word.

Heaven is not a by-product for my faith. I do what I do in life for the eternal kingdom. If I lose sight of this or am not aware of it, I will miss the mark. I can conquer this fallen world and live with a guarantee that the kingdom of God will reign eternally and supremely with no rival and no threat (I Corinthians 15:2-28). This is possible through Jesus Christ's death, resurrection and ascension. I will be sustained through his grace "for thine is the kingdom, and the power and the glory" (Matthew 6:10). I have to become preoccupied with eternity and heaven.

Heaven is my all-consuming point of reference. I have to reflect on the eternal kingdom's values and live them out on this earth.

My roots have to be based on eternity and not on earthly things (John 3:2). My home is heaven. Confidence and courage will drive me forward to conquer in this world because my faith is grounded in eternal values.

Fellowship is the key emphasis and is provided by a God who is true and whose promises are sure. Jesus Christ spent forty days here in his eternal bodily form and then disappeared into the world to come. Biblical hope is established on God's promises. It is easy to believe because I enter every day into fellowship with his indwelling presence. It is a growing process.

Fellowship produces security. It is sure. I have an inner assurance that perseveres with eager anticipation (Romans 8:24, 25). Things may get tough but I have trust that Jesus Christ has provided. I trust God to keep his Word. He has in the past and present and will continue in the future. I will be with him some day (John 14:3).

Fellowship provides fulfillment. It fills the emptiness and despair of the soul. It gives life meaning and direction. It provides for that inner drive to hold onto something secure. It brings excitement to life's adventures and satisfaction in the journey.

Fellowship develops my relationship with Jesus Christ. My life on earth is only a fleeting moment. Eternity is forever. I will sit at his feet as he unfolds the mysteries and miracles of both the macro and the micro elements of his marvelous, wise and intricate design.

Fellowship increases confidence. Sometimes death is fearful. I have to learn to embrace it because the fact is that dying is gain. I am encouraged as I die to self on this earth. This prepares me for heaven. I believe that heaven is real. As I affirm that truth in the depths of my soul. I will be free to live for Christ, even it if requires earth-side loss (Philippians 3:8, 9).

Fellowship is the key to hope. The resurrection of Christ proves that heaven is real. There is life after death. What can possibly distract me? I live for eternity. The more I make heaven my primary goal, the more I will be transformed. When I am for heaven, I will be contented, satisfied and fulfilled (Colossians 3:1, 2). I maximize my faith when I rely on my fellowship with him. No more struggles with my identity. Living for myself is not pre-eminent. I live for the kingdom to come and the kingdom that is within me. My behavior, attitudes, actions and responses relate to who reigns over me — Jesus Christ.

5

Where Does My Security Lie?

My confidence is secure because I am assured of my relationship with Christ.

Salvation is assured through God's Word (I John 5:11, 12). "And this is the record that God hath given to us eternal life and this life is in his Son. He that hath the Son hath life and he that hath not the Son of God hath not life. These things have I written unto you that believe on the name of the Son of God; that ye may know..."

Salvation is assured through God's Authority (I John 1:12, 13). "But as many as received him, to them gave the power to become the Sons of God, even to them that believe on his name; which were born not of blood, nor of the will of the flesh, not of the will of man, but of God."

Salvation is assured through God's Security (John 10:27-30). "My sheep hear my voice and I know them, and they follow me: And I give unto them eternal life, and they shall never perish, neither shall any man pluck them out of my hand.

Salvation is assured through God's Grace (Ephesians 2:8, 9). "For by grace are ye saved through faith, and that not of yourselves; it is the gift of God, not of works, lest any man should boast."

Salvation is assured through God's Justice (I Peter 3:18). "For Christ also hath one suffered for sins, the just for the unjust, that he might bring us to God, being put to death in the flesh but quickened by the Spirit."

Salvation is assured through God's Love (Romans 5:8). "But God commended his love toward us, in that, while we were yet sinners, Christ died for us."

Salvation is assured through Gods Transformation (2 Corinthians 5:17). "Therefore if any man be in Christ, he is a new creature — old things are passed away and behold all things are become new."

Personal Response

6

What About God's Promises?

I am interested in accepting God's provisions for facing trials. I want to share how Psalm 23 has secured the path for me. It starts with authority that can transform the seeking heart. Deity is suddenly facing me. I can handle anything with God alongside of me. There is no losing of ground when I know in whom I believe. I have a growing intimate relationship. "The Lord is my Shepherd." It is hard to comprehend or believe but I have communication with God my creator-sustainer-redeemer and Lord.

There is no deficiency in my life. He provides the promise, "I shall not be in want." Contentment can settle me. Only he can provide such rest and peace. He is in charge and the controller of all things. The unknown is directed by his hand of mercy. This is only the beginning.

I am able to shout and jump with joy because an infinite, holy, self-existent God in whom I have found has provided the way.

The flies and parasites that torment sheep can be found in fear, tension, worry uncertainty and the unknown for humans. Panic, discontent, agitation and restlessness do not have to conquer me. I am going to put his provisions into action. The Scripture says, "Be still and know that I am God" (Psalm 46:10). I have to learn to be quiet. Quietness for some is a way of life. It can be a time to reflect, a time to create, a time to recover, a time to grieve, a time to rejoice or a time to listen to God. I have to put aside the barriers, schedules, outside interruptions and intrusions. Spiritual intimacy is a must. I think activities and the busyness of life have caused me to get off the right track at times. I have to close my eyes and lay down in the green pastures. As I lay down, I reflect in the fact that God the Father chose me in Christ before the foundations of the world (Ephesians 1:4). He predestined me to be adopted as his own (v5).

I reflect on the fact that God the Son carried out God's plan of redemption by shedding his blood on the cross. He redeemed me through his blood and provided forgiveness for my sins (v7). I reflect on the fact that God the Spirit will enable me to respond in faith to God's love and has guaranteed my inheritance (v 13,14). This reflecting brings peace and security. This will help bring freedom from the unknown.

God says, "wait on me — I will renew your strength, don't run and be weary, don't faint but walk in the Spirit" (Isaiah 40:31). I know that God will be with me. He is alive and present whether I feel his presence or not. He will not abandon me. He says "wait on me." I have to rely on him and look to him for my source of strength. Psalm 23 provides what I need to succeed. I do not have to carry the burden of the unknown. God says, give me your burdens, tell me about them, give me your worries and concerns. When I do, I am like the eagle (Isaiah 40:31). As he floats effortlessly in the wind, I can do the same because the unknown is placed into God's hands.

As I learn to be in a resting mode, my mind and heart will hold onto the truth of God's Word. My thirst is quenched though his Word. As I allow it to saturate my mind, my soul becomes relaxed with his presence. His thoughts take control of my spirit. It starts with my spirit, then enters my soul and finally takes charge of my body. I have to learn to disallow the pollution of evil to enter my mind as I drink. The Scriptures will become my measuring rod to test everything. My quiet time becomes a restful, reflective and refueling experience. As I drink of the cool waters, it gives refreshing nourishment. I am putting his provisions into action. I can handle unknown issues in my life because God is equipping me through the Holy Spirit.

I am obtaining rest through recognition that God is giving the rest and a sense of well-being. As I affirm who he is and that he is in me, he produces the rest. I will follow him beside the quiet waters. I am not going to drink the dirty water that surrounds or creeps into the back door of my mind, but the pure water that flows from his Word. My thirst will be quenched because the Holy Spirit is doing the leading. I live in a confused and sick society. Christ comes quietly and invites me to come to him. He knows my heart, personality and soul. He has the capacity to satisfy. Only the Spirit and life of Christ himself will make me complete.

There are many valleys I have crept through. I have learned to put the previous provisions into action. Now I can turn to the most intimate part of the Psalm — "the shadow of death." The sheep face dangers of rampaging rivers, avalanches, rock slides, poisonous plants and predators. I am fortunate to walk in the shadow of the Almighty. Jesus Christ has conquered death. I don't have to be air-lifted out of the situation. In every situation, in every dark trial, in every disappointment, in every distressing dilemma, I walk with the King. Every mountain has its valleys. The walk may be slow but it can be steady with Jesus. Intimate contact with Christ is the key. He says that he is with me. I have to learn to have an attitude of quiet acceptance of every adversity. Through the adversity, I can move to higher ground.

My heart is full of thanksgiving when I realize God has given me a rod and staff to comfort me. The rod or club protects me. The rod becomes the extension of my arm. It is a symbol of strength, power and authority in any serious situation. The rod speaks of the Word of God. It implies the authority of Divinity. The staff provides care. The staff is a symbol of concern and compassion. It is an instrument of patience and kindness. The shepherd leans on it. It is a symbol of the Holy Spirit. The Holy Spirit will guide me, teach me, give understanding, give gentle promptings and counsel me. My reinforcement is provided through the Holy Spirit's constant presence and the use of Scripture against the enemy.

This power comes through his guidance, instruction, understanding and gentle prompting. It is possible when I become intimate with Jesus Christ. Life can be complicated and cluttered. The Scripture calls for simplicity (Ecclesiastes 7:29). Cultivating intimacy with the Almighty will involve a changed life routine. Absolute silence has to follow the simplicity (Psalm 46:10). I have to make time for God. The picture is stillness, quietness, listening and waiting before him. This takes discipline but is indispensable if I hope to add depth to my spiritual life and be reinforced. There is no quick fix in becoming intimate with God. In my solitude, God does the examining (Psalm 139:1-4; 23,24). I have to do the confessing (I John 1:9). When I get rid of the complications of life, I am able to find a time for silence. In my silence, I am able to listen to God and make the adjustments. This will provide serenity in the soul. All these activities will bring me to complete trust (Proverbs 3:5,6). No longer am I preoccupied with working on the details in my life. Unqualified reliance in the living Lord takes place.

My life will have days of gladness and sadness. It will experience delightful days and dark days. I still have a great, sovereign, gracious and good shepherd who provides for me even in the midst of my enemies. He anoints my head with oil. He cares for the sheep and he cares for me. The overflowing presence of the Holy Spirit is continually overshadowing me. Coping with unknown issues turns into contentment when my conscious thought life becomes anointed by the Holy Spirit. I can be free from the world's contamination through faith and acceptance. Just as I have asked Christ to come into my life initially, I need to invite the Holy Spirit to come into my mind to monitor my thought life.

God provides all the preparations to help me. He knows ahead of time my needs. I am blessed with the understanding that he is in charge (sovereignty). I am blessed with experiencing his goodness (grace). I am blessed with his love (mercy). I am blessed with his sufficiency (abundance). I am blessed with his resources (filling). These give me reassurance of his greatness, graciousness and goodness directed toward me.

As I learn to rely on God, his goodness and mercy will pursue me and I will always be at home with him. "I will never leave you nor forsake you" (Hebrews 15:5). I have a privileged position. No matter what comes, my treatment will be with goodness, mercy and his presence. I may have limited knowledge, understanding, wisdom and comprehension but I have an inner witness of the Holy Spirit. He provides confidence as I work through the provision of rest, refreshment, restoration, right-thinking, reinforcement, reassurance and reliance. No disaster, difficulty or dilemma will take charge of my spirit, soul and body. My serenity has its basis on a total reliance on God's ability to do the right thing and the best thing in any given situation for me.

7

Who Will Help Me Practice the Promises?

The indwelling of the Holy Spirit (I Corinthians 6:19) will help me activate the promises in my life. I cannot see him but his personality and presence are facts. His personality is proved in John 16:13, 14. It is hard to handle the unknown but with a counselor and helper like the Holy Spirit, I am able to succeed.

To succeed, I have to follow his leadership. When my heart is touched by him I have to respond. When his words make an impression in my mind, I must act. I have to practice repentance with honesty. I have to practice trust with loyalty. I have to practice obedience with love.

In my late teens, I wrote a little booklet entitled, "A Touch of Heaven on Earth." I believe now, many years later, in the same things I wrote. If I want God's touch, I have to do what he wants. I have to learn daily to be sensitive to the Holy Spirit's presence. I have to stop resisting the Spirit. I have to stop saying no to his guidance. I have to stop refusing to yield to the Word of God as he brings it home to me. I have to be in a constant attitude of yieldedness rather than rebellion. I have to learn to stop sinning against the Spirit. I grieve the Holy Spirit when I break fellowship with him. Unconfessed sin has to be dealt with on a daily basis. I am not dealing with a force or power or influence, but with a person. The Bible says, "As ye have therefore received Christ Jesus the Lord, so walk ye in him" (Colossians 2:6). I received him by faith and the only way victory is obtained is in my dependence upon the Holy Spirit. He dwells in me and my heart has to be emptied of me and filled with him. The question is, Am I dominated by the Holy Spirit or by myself? Having a "touch of heaven" is through meeting certain conditions; stop resisting the Spirit, stop sinning against the Spirit and stop walking in the flesh.

Right at the time I think all is well, it seems everything will fall apart. The enemy knows my weaknesses. He certainly does not want me to bring glory to the Lord Jesus Christ. I cannot let my guard down. I have to realize that a battle is going on. At all times, I have to stand ready with offensive and defensive weapons.

I can face defeat. I can feel cast down. I can be distressed. I may be frustrated and experienced helplessness. I can even enter into depression. The struggles can be big in my eyes but not in God's eyes. I have to keep focused on him and when I take my eyes off of him, I will sink. Let's keep in mind that Jesus is a caring shepherd. In my spiritual dilemma, he doesn't become disgusted or fed up. I have experienced his love, compassion and tender care. He is ready to give reassurances, patience and restoration. In the path of life, there are many dangers. Restoration takes place when I am free of myself. God knows what he is doing with me. He is in charge. I am glad that he is ready to restore my soul.

I am glad God is ready to restore even when I have missed the mark. Sometimes I have forgotten that a battle is going on. As a musician-trumpeter, I have played "Sound the Battle Cry!" many times. Verse three says, "O Thou God of all, hear us when we call, help us one and all by thy grace; when the battle's done and the victory won, may we wear the crown before thy face." It seems suddenly in the midst of a calm, ordered and peaceful life, all the forces of Satan can break loose. He restores me through giving me understanding of the threefold attack. The act of creation is described as follows: "And the Lord God formed man of the dust of the ground and breathed into his nostrils the breath of life; and man became a living soul" (Genesis 2:7). The Scripture reveals that the body was made of the dust of the ground, that the spirit came from the breath of God and that the combination produced the soul (Hebrews 4:12). Satan's mind works against the spirit, soul and body of men. Against the body, he brings the temptations of the flesh. Against the soul, he brings the temptation of the world. Against the spirit, he comes himself or through one of his lesser agents.

I am not a casualty in the warfare. I can learn the subtle devices of the enemy, the devil. Let me begin with the flesh or body. I am not referring to the soft substance of the living body which covers the bones and is penetrated with blood. The body has a proper use of its every function and is normal, natural and moral. There is no sin involved or anything in connection with the human body itself. There is a human side apart from divine influence and it is prone to sin and oppose God. The body cannot run the affairs of the spirit and soul. It has to be controlled by the spirit and soul. When my will chooses to allow my body to dictate what it is going to do, then something is wrong. I am to abstain from anything that is in contrast to the principles of God's Word. I have to be so familiar with his Word that I will know what is right or wrong for me to do. It is not a bunch of rules but applied principles. Run from the enemy. The crucifixion of self has to take place. The enemy attacks the soul with the influence of the world. My senses are the focus. Whatever is drawing me away from the will of God is wrong to follow. If it keeps me away from Jesus, something is wrong. I cannot conform to the world's ideas. Conforming to the image of God's Son will show me what it means to not conform to the world.

Faith is the key word to build upon (I John 5:4), a definite turning away from the world "set eternity in the heart" (Ecclesiastes 3:11). Faith is a daily decision to respond to his Word in the correct way. The devil's greatest interest is my spirit. The sins of the body and conformity to the world are terrible in themselves but the denial of God in the heart is unpardonable. Submission to God is absolutely necessary. Resisting comes next and putting on the armor of God will bring deliverance. In leaning on my own understanding (spirit-sin), I will fail to rest in the Lord with my whole heart (soul-sin) and will allow weakness in the body to flourish (flesh-sin).

Learning to cooperate with the Holy Spirit is the major focus. My spirit and soul need to be in line with God's will. He makes this possible by his own gracious Spirit who is given to those who obey (Acts 5:32). For it is he who works in us both to will and to do of his good pleasure (Philippians 2:13).

8

What is the Preparation in Accepting the Promises?

Prayer is the divine arrangement that God has made to communicate with him. I had to learn to leap out into the unknown. I had to accept and act on his promises. I had to submit to his will and accept his answers. I had to reject any thoughts that hinder my submissive attitude. I had to practice the presence of God. I had to take him at his Word and to accept the challenges. I had to accept my circumstances in life realizing God will do what is good for me and never do what is bad for me. I had to confess my wrongdoing and accept his cleansing. I had to learn that my daily activities are directed by God's sovereignty and majesty. I had to learn to focus on Jesus, not the situation, and to learn that everything is in his lap.

As I have been in the process of learning these things, several activities have taken place in my life. Transformation in my behavior has taken place and a restful spirit with daily affirmations to God's promises has taken place. The gaps in faith have been reduced to the past. I am ready to learn how to "pray in the Spirit" Ephesians 6:8). I am ready to "pray continually" (1 Thessalonians 5:17). I am ready to ask whatever I wish and it shall be done for me (John 15:7). I am ready to become the righteous man whose prayer availeth much (James 5:16). I have joined the disciples in saying "Lord, teach us to pray" (Luke 11:1). Communicating with God is not mystical or mysterious. It is not a trivial religious expression nor just an elementary exercise in asking and receiving. In our humanity, we get side-tracked into thinking only about ourselves. Praying is the way that the life of God in us is nourished. When we read the Bible, God talks to us and we are fed. Both responses bring development. Scriptural study and talking to God will change our inner nature. An intimate relationship with God will take place.

What is the Preparation in Accepting the Promises?

Several years ago, my family was in a head-on car collision. It threw us into the ditch against a tree. The day was ugly with ice and snow. There were several other accidents on the same street also that day. The emergency crew was already on the site so we had immediate help. They worked on the car doors to get us out. Amazingly, we were not hurt but do have some psychological reminders.

About a month later, a second car was demolished with another head-on collision. Neither of the two accidents were my family's fault. There were some miracles that took place during this accident in that our daughter-in-law was pregnant so there was great concern for her and the baby. They both came through the accident safely. A second miracle took place when the car rolled over and all the windows were broken on the opposite side of the car that our daughter and grandson were sitting. They were saved from being cut. A third miracle took place when everyone walked away from the accident in shock and upset but all in one piece.

Praise the Lord! After these two experiences, I began praying the Lord's Prayer on a daily basis. Every day when I get into my car, I have talked to God through that prayer. It is my model and direction in life and has become a part of my very being. It has been fun discussing each word with God. Each time that I pray the prayer, I obtain new insights from it. My day is entered with excitement and joy because it starts with God's counsel.

9

What Enables Me to Experience the Promises?

I have a tremendous privilege in talking to God. If I accept, a radical lifestyle could appear for me. God does not give promises that he will not keep. The problem is my neglect of prayer and understanding the truths that relate to it. He is wise, powerful and faithful enough to do what he has said. I have to follow Jesus' example and withdraw myself to a quiet place (Luke 5:15, 16).

I have enablement through the redeeming work of the Lord Jesus Christ. Every provision has been made so I can live in fellowship with God and pray (Ephesians 2:12, 18). I have access to God because of my faith in Jesus Christ (John 14:6). This relationship is solid and steadfast. Praying is a dominant characteristic of my life.

I can come to him, talk to him and present my request and receive an answer.

Praying is a personal and private meeting with God. It is the foundation to build upon and will teach us the intercessory form of prayer. I need to pray with the expectation that things will happen as I make my request known. He will reward me openly because I have learned to pray in his will (1 John 5:14, 15). To pray in his will, I have to realize and act upon the fact that I am identified in the death and resurrection of Jesus Christ. In the crucifixion, I was set free from the bondage and defilement of sin. In the resurrection I have been given the enablement to live above sin. Jesus has accomplished this for me. I am buried with him and raised with him (Romans 6:4, 6).

I have enablement through the Holy Spirit (Ephesians 6:18). The Holy Spirit has been given to me. He will teach me and enable me to pray. It is almost beyond my comprehension to get ahold of this fact but it does happen. I am able to pray and have amazing results because the Holy Spirit has come to apply the work of the Lord Jesus in my life through the Word of God. This is why it is essential that I understand the meaning of redemption and make realistic choices to obey God (John 16:13, 14). I have to learn to recognize the patterns of sin and the patterns of holiness. I have to break down the old and then a new pattern can be established by divine help. "Put off the old behavior and put on the new" (Ephesians 4:22, 24). When this is accomplished on a daily basis, I will pray in God's will and see things happen.

No name is greater than that of Jesus Christ and he gives me the right to pray in his name. This is the highest authority that is possible in heaven and earth. To be able to present my request in his name means total acceptance by God. Praying with his authority means that I am in agreement with him in everything.

I have enablement through representing others to Jesus. He provides the wisdom. The new priesthood offers sacrifices through Jesus Christ and they are spiritual. I have a responsibility to live with the blessing as an heir of his salvation. I need to give my body to him as a living sacrifice (Romans 12:1,2) as well as the praise of my lips (Hebrews 13:15) and the good works (13:16). Money and other material things I share with others in God's service are also spiritual sacrifices (Philippians 4:10-20). God enables me to pray through his invitation to call on him by being redeemed by Jesus, having the Holy Spirit's guidance through Jesus, praying in Jesus' name and representing others to Jesus Christ.

Betty is a single parent and has retired from a long career as an Emergency Room nurse. She has a love for children and decided to adopt. Four children arrived on her doorstep by way of India. This has become a delightful adventure with ups and downs in a path of uncertainty and planned objectives took place. Today she is facing a serious illness and has gone through surgery, treatment, therapy and the unknown. It seems every day brings the necessity of God's presence. She has many questions like; what do I do about this issue or that circumstance, how is God going to work it all out and I really don't know what to do? Betty says, 'I know I have to let go and just let God do it — I am doing the best I can — why do things in life seem to go backward?' She is a soul-caring person so she takes on herself many other struggling peoples' needs. She is learning to be enabled by God's presence.

10

What Unlocks the Promises for Me?

Many years ago I memorized John 16:24 to give me assurance that God hears and responds to my communication. I need to turn my heart to God until my subconscious mind is continually in touch with him. God says that he hears my prayers (Psalm 65). Where there is a hunger, God wants to satisfy it. "Every good gift and every perfect gift is from above and cometh down from the Father of lights with whom is no variableness, neither shadow of turning" (James 1:7). His loving concern is about whatever want or desire or need my searching heart has. He is a rewarder of them that diligently seek him (Hebrews 11:6).

I want to be limitless in the possibilities of prayer. The infinite Almighty God is able to give great answers to prayer. He is the Creator and Sustainer of all things. God is able to give "all things" to his own (Romans 8:32). The little and big requests are at his fingertips. He is ready to give an answer.

Receiving depends upon my commitment. Have I committed myself to Jesus' name? These words are very plain, very simple, very positive and precious. To pray in his name means I have believed and trusted my soul to him. I do not believe about Jesus but I believe in Jesus. A transformation has taken place. In John 1:12, I have the authority to pray in his name. I have accepted his claims and have a relationship with him. My life is committed to him. I have a living faith in Jesus and an obedient love. My entire conduct is under his control because I am committed to him. To pray in Jesus' name means that I agree with Jesus and what Jesus says about whatever I am praying for. It is not just using his name at the end of the prayer. Drawing near to God is the response. I have no claims on God. Only through Jesus' name, I have the privilege to bow before him with my request.

Receiving depends upon my condition. The impression that many people have is that all the promises in the Word of God in regard to his answering prayer are made to everyone and that anyone can claim these promises. God's promises are made to certain specified people. I have to examine my condition and ask do I keep his commandments? God demands that I listen to his Word before he will listen to my prayers. Do not turn a deaf ear to his commands. I must study the Scriptures diligently each day to find out what his will is and then I have to do it. This is not mysterious. The foundation for praying has to be grounded in his Word. My condition has to be in an attitude of love and obedience. The Holy Spirit will guide "according to the will of God" (John 14:13, 14). It is not enough that I keep the commandments, but I must do the things that please him. The challenge is to get thoroughly acquainted with God so that I know instinctively what will please God and what will displease him.

Receiving depends upon my confidence in Jesus Christ (1 John 5:14-16). I must pray with a confident expectation of getting the very things that I ask. It is the confidence that I have in him and not based upon the degree of faith I have, but on the person who is the object of my faith – God. I can pray with no doubt that God will hear the prayer and grant the specific thing I have asked for. When I pray to God and pray according to his will which is found in his promises, I can confidently believe that the very thing I have asked is granted to me. I have to believe that I have received and will personally experience it (Mark 11:24).

To pray with confidence (faith), I have to study his Word and find out what he has definitely promised. Is there a promise that covers my request? Than I can rest upon the promise and believe that God has heard what I asked for. I have to learn to hear his voice in my heart through his Word and submit my spirit, soul and body to him.

How can I pray so as to get what I ask? If I am committed to Jesus, if I keep his commands and if I have confidence, I have the foundation to get started (James 4:2). The seven words in this Scripture give the challenge. Receiving depends upon my asking. I think that this may be an age of anxiety and tolerance or add your own words. The most important word would be prayerlessness. Praying is beneficial to many as a 'reflex influence.' I pray when I am in stress or facing something difficult. It should be a regular part of my life. Prevailing prayer should be the theme of life. Praying unlocks all the storehouses of God's infinite grace and power. God's ear is quick to hear the voice of real praying. The Lord God omnipotent works for me and works through me (James 5:16). The "righteous man" is described as a man living out the fruit of the Spirit every day (Galatians 5:22, 23). Spiritual maturity is discovered when the Holy Spirit's indwelling presence and power is manifested.

This past week I met a man that prevails in prayer. It is not a reflex influence. It is a necessity not only for physical needs but for the spiritual warfare that is going on. I wrote "the Lord God omnipotent works for me and works through me." I believe that Chuck is an example of this. He has a lung disease with most of his lung being removed. At one time the doctors gave him up and asked his family to say good-by. Even a death certificate was being completed but suddenly he came back to life. He does not qualify for a transplant because of the rules of cancer, age, etc. The thing that keeps him going he says is, "God is in control and I'm learning to depend upon him for everything." God has given me his perspective for living and dying. I have no fear. God has given me the gift of faith; my job is to continue to pray. I cannot do anything else but this is sufficient. It is the most important thing to do. Praying without ceasing is my desire.

Do I Have Pure Motives in Regard to the Promises?

I can open the door to a more powerful relationship with God through the foundational, relational, instructional and spiritual sections of my book if I have pure motives. Pure motives can be generated through fasting and this will take private discipline. It will involve intimacy and will show sincerity. It will involve craving for God's Word. It will provide cleansing and will be manifested through supernatural power. I have heard the word 'fasting' many times during my sickness. Several medical tests at the hospital have caused a positive response through fasting. The physical side of fasting has been a cleansing resource.

Jesus spent time in prayer and fasting (Luke 4:1, 2). He is my model. Biblical fasting is refraining from food for a spiritual purpose. Pure motives are my spiritual purpose. Fasting keeps me sensitive to the Holy Spirit which will enable me to live a holy life. This is my sacrifice (Romans 12:1). He knows my next assignment and will bless me as I draw near to him. Pure motives are produced through knowing that the enemy is defeated. His agenda is to steal, kill and destroy (John 10:10). He knows he is defeated but doesn't want me to know it or to walk with God's indwelling. Pure motives can be achieved through a hunger for God's presence. He knows more about me than I do. Breaking through any situation is possible. "Taste and see that the Lord is good" (Psalm 34:8).

Pure motives will abound when I believe God. The birthplace of faith is found in "hearing the Word of God" (Romans 10:17). If the Scripture truly takes hold of my spirit, I will never allow the devil to talk me out of being faithful "His words will never pass away" (Mark 13:31). Fasting can be a means to obtain pure motives. The innermost part of my being has to be in touch with the divine. He will peel off the layers of my spirit, soul and body that are necessary. Intense prayer, repentance, soul searching and a thankful heart will create the way to pure motives.

Do the Promises Bring Security?

During the dark days in my journey, my son immediately gave me a verse from Hosea 6:3 "Let us acknowledge the Lord . . . as surely as the sun rises he will appear . . . he will come to us." My daughter shared Psalm 91:1 "He who dwells in the shelter of the most High will rest in the shadow of the Almighty." Both Bible references reinforced the verse the Holy Spirit gave to me and my wife, James 4:8 "Draw near to God and he will draw near to you."

In the first two sections of this book, I have learned how to 'draw near to God.' His presence has become real. I have security in his promises because he gives me a sense of his presence and love. To understand God's love, I have to know God's eternal passion to accomplish his will in such a way that he is glorified. God's love is eternal.

God was love before he created man or anything else. I have to learn to let God be God. His will and glory go hand in hand to produce his love. I am under his umbrella of love. He unfolds his will to achieve his glory in my life through love.

I must learn to take every circumstance of life and glorify him. The challenge is to be consumed with his love. I must keep his purpose in mind and then inner strength will flow. He gives me a sense of his presence and grace. I do not deserve grace but God has given it to me. It is his unmerited favor. Grace is designed to save and keep me. The Scripture says, "Grow in the grace and knowledge of our Lord and Savior Jesus Christ" (2 Peter 3:18). God is sufficient. God's grace is his empowerment to overcome. It raises me above the problem and gives me power at the exact point when I want to quit. Grace instructs me in how to live. Grace gives victory where I didn't have it. Grace will give the ability to keep going. Grace is the exchanging of my life for Christ (Galatians 2:20). Grace is inner spiritual power and not outward religious conformity. I have been set free to enjoy Christ's life in me (Galatians 5:1). I am challenged to measure my growth in grace; if I am lacking, I ask for his grace.

God gives me a sense of his presence and sovereignty. He has absolute rule and control over all of creation. This means he causes or allows everything. I have to put everything in life under that perspective. It certainly makes me think, act and live different. He has created and owns everything. He can do as he pleases. Everything that occurs does so under the hand of a sovereign God. There are no chance happenings, no luck and no mistakes. Good and bad fall under his control. God knows where he is going and allows me to make choices. He will achieve his intended purpose which is to receive glory. I exist to please him (2 Timothy 2:4). I obtain strength through him (Philippians 4:13). I have confidence in him (2 Timothy 1:12).

He gives me a sense of his presence and glory. God's inner core is a radiating light (1 Timothy 6:15, 16). God's visible glory was most fully seen in the person of Jesus Christ who is God in the flesh (Matthew 17:1-8). I am to tell of his glory. His glory will put a glow in my life. Transformation is a growing adventure. I have to learn to submit to God's glory (1 Corinthians 10:31).

He gives me a sense of his presence and justice. God is good, kind, loving and forgiving. He is also just and I must take his wrath seriously. God must judge sin because of the justice of his law and the righteousness of his character. He takes no pleasure in punishing the unrighteous (Ezekiel 33:11). He will judge all men according to their deeds (1 Peter 1:17). The word 'wrath' indicates God's intense displeasure of sin. God's wrath is not cruel but just. There are two sides to God's response to sin. "Thou hast loved righteousness and hated wickedness" (Psalm 45:7). I am glad that God is patient (2 Peter 3:9). My only way of escape is through God's substitute, Jesus who "delivers me from the wrath to come" (1 Thessalonians 1:10). Christ died for me (Romans 5:8, 9).

He gives me a sense of his presence and wisdom. Wisdom is knowing that God's purpose is to glorify himself. Wisdom moves all events, all people and all circumstances toward his purpose. Whether I resist or cooperate, he is still going to achieve his purpose. Wisdom is the ability to use my spiritual character, Biblical knowledge, common sense and circumstances and blending them together. I have an infinitely wise God who has been ordering my life. I was in his mind before the creation of the earth. He will give wisdom to make the response that will bring him glory. A determined will to agree with 'thy will be done' is the answer. Ask in faith and anticipate the answer. Mixing human wisdom and divine wisdom does not work (James 3:16-18). To obtain wisdom, I have to admit that I need it. I have to stand in awe of God. I have to study the Word. I need to pray for wisdom (James 1:5). He gives me a sense of his presence and grace.

God says, "... I will draw near to you." When I mix scripture and faith together, I will be secure through his promises. His presence has been experienced through love, grace, sovereignty, glory, justice and wisdom.

Personal Response

13

What Makes Me Think That the Bible is Dependable?

As I delight in his law (Scripture), I will be blessed. The promise "Blessed is the man who walketh not in the council of the ungodly ... but his delight is in the law of the Lord" has laid the foundation (Psalm 1:1-2). I grew up believing in the Bible. I am extremely glad that I can say that. I do not take it for granted. I have had to unlearn a few things but the primary fundamental doctrines have been planted well into my brain waves. In those early days, if someone asked me to walk across the lake, I would have believe that God could accomplish it. If you asked why I believe, the answer would simply be that someone did it in the Scriptures. As long as they had their eyes on Jesus, no sinking took place. This belief remains secure because my spirit, soul and body have been entrusted in faith to Jesus Christ.

Everyone has to make a decision about the Bible "the sure word" (2 Peter 1:19). There is no escape. You may cherish, read, ignore, respect, dissect, study or hate it, but a decision has to be made. I began to read in the Bible and reflect on the fact that even though the original was written centuries ago, it is pertinent for me today. The Bible repeatedly speaks in terms that involve all generations. Jesus claimed, "Heaven and earth will pass away, but my words shall not pass away) (Matthew 24:35). The prophet Isaiah said, "The grass withers, the flowers fade, but the Word of our God stands forever" (Isaiah 40:8). It claims within itself to come from an all-knowing, all-powerful, personal God. You can laugh at the Bible and you can think that it is not relevant today. You can be a skeptic, religionist, agnostic, atheist, satanist or just a naïve person with good ethical standards, but the Bible is still for you.

As I was reading it, I couldn't help realize the uniqueness of it. It is different, it is one of a kind, it has no equal, it is a book written over a 1,500-year span and it was written over 40 generations. It was written by more than 40 authors from every walk of life including kings, peasants, philosophers, fishermen, poets, statesmen, scholars and more. It was written in three continents; Asia, Africa and Europe. It was written in three languages; Hebrew, Aramaic and Greek. It covers hundreds of topics. Yet the biblical authors spoke with harmony and continuity from Genesis to Revelation. There is one unfolding story; God's redemption of man.

There are many reasons why the Bible is important to apply to ones life. Its dependability is connected to its uniqueness, the canon, bibliographical test, internal evidence, prophesies fulfilled, historical geography, archeological evidences, miracles and its transforming power. Jesus Christ has made a direct challenge to my will to trust him. He says, "I have been standing at the door and I am constantly knocking. If anyone hears me calling him and opens the door, I will come in (Revelation 3:20). I discovered that when I accepted Jesus Christ as my Savior and believed he died on the cross for me and that he was resurrected, through faith my life has been changed from the inside out. I am convinced that the Bible is dependable because of the divine genius who has put it together. It has fulfilled the promise of blessing.

Holy men from God spoke as they were carried along by the Holy Spirit (2 Peter 1:21). The genius of this record is through the Holy Spirit moving upon, in and through human authors. The translation of God's thoughts and will to humanity is through language and inspiration carried along by the Holy Spirit. The Bible (66 books in the Old and New Testaments) has had a divine intervention. "No prophecy ever resulted from human design" (2 Peter 1:21). "We have a more sure word of prophecy" (2 Peter 1:19). We are not permitted to judge the Bible by our experiences but we must judge our experience by the Bible, 'the sure word.'

I am convinced that the Bible is dependable because of my spiritual understanding. "No prophetic Scripture can be explained by one's unaided mental powers" (2 Peter 1:20). The spiritual origin of the word necessitates spiritual understanding. Natural men cannot receive spiritual truth. The whole concept of scriptural ministry indicates that the minister of the New Testament is "not of the letter, but of the spirit, for the letter killeth but the spirit giveth life" (2 Corinthians 3:6). "It is the spirit that beareth witness because the Spirit is truth" (1 John 5:6). I cannot intellectualize or bargain with God, by faith I understand. The foundation and solid ground is the Holy Scriptures. Anyone can read the Bible but without the Holy Spirit's guided intelligence, the information is worth little. The study of the Word of God brings confidence.

I am convinced that the Bible is dependable because of my relationship with Jesus Christ. "These are written in order that you may believe that Jesus is the Christ, the anointed one, the Son of God and through believing in cleaving to trusting in and relying upon him, you may have life through his name" (John 20:31). The life is in him and not through any religious duties however beautifully performed. It is terrifying to know that this plain word, this testimony of Jesus, can be in a man's possession and he can miss the God of revelation. When we miss Jesus, we miss what God wants us to know. The great aim of the Christian life is not simply to know a set of ethics, but that "I may know him" (Philippians 3:10).

I think that everyone will come to a point in their life that they have to be convinced whether the Bible is true or not. My own mind and heart had to be convinced even though I was trained as a child and young adult. I appreciated my early foundation but I had to learn, decide and discover my own answers. I was in Chicago taking special studies at the American Conservatory of Music. One evening I picked up a book dealing with many reasons why I shouldn't believe in Christianity and the Bible. I had to come to terms with following the Bible all the way, partially or not at all. Satan tried to be deceptive in my mind and the council of the ungodly raised some questions. Amazing as it might sound, because I have delighted in the study of God' Word, the Bible, it began to convince me. Many scriptures came to my mind when my soul was troubled. Jesus said, "Let not your heart be troubled, ye believe in God, believe also in me...I am the way, the truth and the life" (John 14:1, 6). I threw the other book away. It really didn't have solid reasons in it. It just gave testimony of many Christians in the church that have been poor witnesses.

As I was walking on the shore of Lake Michigan and looking into the starlit sky above and the blue waters below, the Holy Spirit reminded me of the Bible verses that I had learned years ago. The witness of divinity and my own spirit were united and I was truly blessed. The council of the ungodly will lead you astray but his Word will bless your life. I believe in the dependability of the Scriptures. They continue to bless me in so many different ways. God's counsel is dependable.

14

Do I Have God's Mindset During Trials?

I hear a lot of talking about health now. When I am with the older set of people, the conversation always refers to some part of the body that is not working well or hurts. When I am with the younger set, the conversation is about what gym they belong to. I like being around my students because the subject does not usually come up and when it does, it is with a positive attitude. The government is talking about health and insurance companies are discussing the cost of health. I would like to share what God says about health sickness and suffering. I have put my arms around Psalm 103:3 where it says "Bless the Lord . . . who heals all the diseases."

The Psalmist starts with "Bless the Lord, O my soul" and concludes with the same words.

The delightful text consists of twenty-two verses, which is the exact number of letters in the Hebrew alphabet. It is a great hymn book of the church. When we are hurting, we must turn our attention to the God who has created us. All our senses and faculties should be placed on blessing the holy name of God. Our innermost self is inflamed when we are suffering and either we will magnify the Lord or reject him. I would rather recount all his benefits. He renews us like the eagles, he performs with his sovereign grace and he has removed our sins.

We have a corruptible body, a death-doomed body. There is the promise of the redemption of the body for which all true believers wait. When the Lord returns, we shall have that redemption changed into his own likeness and our bodies will then be like his glorious body. When we face health issues, let us remember healing is possible if it is in his will. If it is or not, he says, "I am with you" (Psalm 23:4). This brings a sense of confidence. His presence is within us and he has no time or space limits. He encompasses everything and everywhere. "In him we live and move and exist" (Acts 17:28).

His eye keeps us in his sight. His guidance is available. We have to learn to let his instruction flow into our hearts and minds. His negatives are a part of his positive program. He leads even when we feel him or not and he keeps his promise, "I am with you and will keep you wherever you go . . . I will not leave you" (Hebrews 15:5). In sickness we can find assurance that he is near and nothing is out of his knowledge to know.

His victory is close at hand. He will provide a way of escape. This means that he will lead us, give us security, provide strength and enable us to find peace. Wherever we go, God goes. He is in us, around us, over us, under us and beside us (1 Corinthians 10:13). He knows our needs and will supply (Philippians 4:19). He will wipe the tears for he sees us (Genesis 16:6). The provisions that are needed are in his fingertips ready for action. We do not have to be anxious or fearful. He is the freedom giver. He surrounds us (Isaiah

41:10). He says, "I will help you, I will strengthen you I will uphold you."

"Your suffering is not in vain, it has a purpose" (1 Peter 2:19-21). Just at the moment of need, he is present on the scene. He provides protection and will carry us through. Sometimes it may seem that he is not near but as we focus or even when we cannot, he says "I will guard your heart and mind" (Philippians 4:6, 7). These are loving words that I have recited in my mind over and over again. They will keep us safe, strong and secure. I challenge you when in ill health or a bad circumstance to regain strength through claiming these promises. Stand back and watch God's hand at work. It really does work!

We do not suffer apart from the knowledge of God. Do not be intimated by all the talk. God knows all the details. Think about God's character rather than his creation. He is in control. Let the big picture rule your life, not the suffering. There is no promise of trouble-free living only power to endure the trouble that is inevitable.

"Have mercy upon me O Lord; for I am weak, O Lord, heal me" (Psalm 6:2). God is not against me when I suffer. He cares about me enough to save every one of my tears (Psalm 56:8). Through the tears, "he has heard my supplication the Lord will receive my prayer" (Psalm 6:9). I have confidence that when I have been willing to go to the secret place, the shadow of the Almighty, there will be comfort. Jesus Christ is the secret place of the Most High. Before suffering occurs, I have learned that thinking right is necessary. An ounce of prevention is good to practice. If we think correctly when we are well, the process will fall into action when we are not so well.

A conscious awareness of the Holy Spirit, our helper, is necessary. I have done this through reciting the Lord's Prayer (Matthew 6) and the shepherd Psalm (Psalm 23). As God takes up residence in me, I begin to live in his shadow and experience his hand covering me. Comfort is a result of continuous dwelling in him. His superiority, sovereignty and sufficiency abound and will produce a wave of strength over my suffering. When I cannot see or understand something, God can. My feeling of apprehension, concern, worry, dread and anxiety will come under the shadow of the Almighty. When I recite God's words and dialogue with him I am strengthened. His will will be done and "I shall not want" will bring security. I have learned that God is all powerful all wise, all loving and never changing. I am in his hands. He reminds me that I cannot do it but he can.

Reflecting on the past has produced the reassurance that God has my best interest in mind. I have had to commit the sickness to the Lord through being more aware of him than the illness. I have had to release it to him because he is quite capable of handling it. His word has been implanted in my mind and heart. A daily breathing in of the Holy Spirit is absolutely necessary.

God's presence was at my birth. Three babies that were unexpected were born at home in a small upstairs apartment during a cold winter storm. Some premature issues followed but God's hand was present. It was an amazing God-touched miracle. God's presence was unique in my childhood. I was running to school and took a short cut. I came head on with a car as I turned the corner. The driver did not see me and I did not see the car coming. I tried to get out of the way but the gravel under my feet made me fall. The front wheels of the car came to a screeching halt right next to my lower back. Did an angel stop those wheels from rolling over me?

God's presence was seen in my teens. During an act of kindness, my hands were infected. The doctors tried medicine, radiation and acid. I could feel the acid eat away the infection. The Holy Trinity provided aid. My one hand was held by Jesus and the other by the Holy Spirit. The heavenly Father gave me a sense of his presence.

God's presence was experience in my adulthood. I was standing by the pulpit of my church. I would imagine the people in their favorite seats as I rehearsed my Sunday sermon. Suddenly I had a lot of pain and dropped my Bible and fell to the floor. I had experienced a silent heart attack. The doctor determined what to do. I witnessed God's intervention.

Relying on God's promises brings abundant living even in suffering. "My hope is in Jesus. Hear my prayer, O Lord, listen to my cry for help" (Psalm 39:7, 12). There is no one whose understanding of life has come close to his. He will help us. I am learning that when I think correctly, it will involve reciting God's Word. This leads to reflecting on personal experiences. Reciting and reflecting will climax in reliance. Reliance on God's promises will bring rest, courage, strength and expected hope.

15

How Do I Saturate My Thoughts With God's?

The more I think upon God's Word, the more I will think like God. His view of things will become my views and his attitudes will become mine. Knowing God's will causes me to pray in his will. It is exciting to explore the vastness of an infinite God. It is also exciting to see how I am wonderfully made (Psalm 139:14). Through my situation, I am more conscious of how the brain and heart work. The situation and the knowledge of God must be transferred to the heart. The brain and heart oversee complex systems that are necessary for life, the nervous system and the circulatory system. Each is encased in a protective fortress of calcium, one inside the cranium and the other within the rib cage. They are on the job all the time with no days off until death or the resurrection day. The human brain is the single most complex apparatus of all God's vast creative genius. It is the center of my nervous system and contains billions of neurons, each having thousands of synoptic connections.

The heart is smaller than my brain but no less impressive. In an average lifetime, the heart contracts and relaxes two and a half billion times without stopping to rest. In every heart, blood is drawn into my heart, filtered, processed and pumped back out again to every millimeter of my body. The brain is the center of my thinking and the heart represents my affection, emotion and personality. I have to learn to love the Lord with all my heart and to keep my heart with all diligence for out of it springs the issues of life (Proverbs 4:23). Sometimes it is hard to get the message from head to heart.

The knowledge of God has to filter down into the heart. It takes nourishment from God's Word through observation, interpretation and application. I have to inform my thinking through contemplation. I will then understand his perspectives. I am all set as I respond to the text, "What think ye of Christ" (Matthew 22:42). I am learning to be a doer of the Word (James 1:22). This is absolutely necessary for me. My heart stopped pumping blood as a matter of fact during surgery. A life machine kept it pumping. After four bypasses and some valve work, it started to work on its own again. The nervous system, circulatory system, rib cage and the emotions and personality have all been affected. I discovered that the supernatural power of God can be infused in me through the Holy Spirit. The saturating of God's Word through accepting its authority, applying it and studying it will make me think like God.

The Bible says, "And he reasoned in the synagogue and persuaded the Jews and Greeks, and he continued teaching the Word of God among them" (Acts 18:4, 11). I know of no other way to give the authority of the Scriptures than to continue teaching the word. I would like to reason and persuade you that the Scriptures are a living, vital agency with supernatural power in itself. Read the promise, "For as the rain cometh down and the snow from heaven, and returneth not thither, but watereth the earth and maketh it bring forth and bud, that it may give seed to the sower and bread to the eater; so shall my word be that goeth forth out of my mouth. It shall not return unto me void, but it shall accomplish that which I please, and it shall prosper in the thing whereto I sent it" (Isaiah 55:10, 11). To the same purpose Jeremiah has written, "Is not my word like as a fire? saith the Lord; and like a hammer that breaketh the rock in pieces?" (Jeremiah 23:29). God uses his word, "For the word of God is quick and powerful and sharper than any two-edged sword, piercing even to the dividing asunder of soul and spirit and of the joints and marrow, and is a discerner of the thoughts and intents of the heart" (Hebrews 4:12).

The Bible is an ancient book for modern times. It is one book, one history and one story and one mind produced it. God himself became a man so that we might know what to think when we think of God. I could give all the evidences for scriptural authority but why don't you read the Bible for yourself and let it prove itself? The Bible says, "As newborn babes, desire the sincere milk of the word, that ye may grow thereby" (1 Peter 2:2). God has given his word so that believers may grow thereby. We have not fulfilled out obligations to the word until application has taken place. The Bible is not only the source book for information but has life changing power for today. Growth in the spiritual life comes not merely from hearing but from hearing and doing. The Bible says, "the effectual doer shall be blessed in what he does" (James 1:25). "If you know these things, you are blessed if ye do them" (John 12:17).

The Bible has been given so that man's basic nature can be changed. "All scripture is given by God and is profitable for teaching, for reproof for correction, for training in righteousness, that the man of God may be adequate, equipped for every good work" (2 Timothy 3:16, 17). It teaches, rebukes, restores and trains for righteous living.

It equips us to do the work that God wants us to do. The Bible convicts, regenerates, nurtures, cleanses, counsels, guides, prevents sin, revives, strengthens, gives wisdom, delivers and helps. The Bible alone realistically and sufficiently meets man's deepest problems, longings, needs and inadequacies. It provides the answers to man's needs for deliverance from the penalty of sin, for spiritual progress for victory, for guidance and for personal relationships and conduct. As we learn the Scriptures, let us apply it to our daily activities

The Bible says, "Blessed are the undefiled in the way, who walk in the law of the Lord" (Psalm 119:1). What is wrong with reading the Bible? Why do people think it so strange? Some people have the idea that the Bible is just for the mentally weak, for the ignorant and some imagine that it just for the shut-ins or only for the children. Why do the teens and young adults turn from it? I believe they do not go on to read it, believe it, study it or follow it. If we are going to walk in the law of the Lord, we must follow this pattern.

We need to study it through and master a verse every day. Think of it and at the end of the year, you will have 365 verses in your heart and mind to bring about happiness, direction, peace and contentment. We need to pray about it. We must let each verse become a part of our very being, praying the verse into reality and then seeing the promises of God, as we claim them, change our lives. We must write down our thoughts. We cannot remember everything but our computer mind has it and we need to refresh our memory. That, of course, brings us to working it out. Let the Bible get in your heart and then live it out every day. It is not good only to study it through or pray about it or put it down or work it out, but we must also pass it on. We must talk about it. Let the Word of God inspire and bless your heart. This takes discipline. You cannot be lazy. Walk in the law of the Lord and you will be saturated with his thoughts.

16

How Do I Apply God's Instruction to My Daily Activities?

I want to share what I practice in order to overcome weakness, trials and troublesome situations. Someone said, 'thinking right always precedes acting right.' To think right means that I have experienced spiritual insight through biblical understanding. When I put Jesus' words into action, I will find contentment and rest. I have to draw near to God (James 4:8). This will involve putting God's perspective on my attitudes toward everything. He gives the instruction and empowerment.

I am learning to be helpless (poor in spirit). Jesus said, "Blessed are the poor in spirit for theirs is the kingdom of heaven" (Matthew 5:3).

Helplessness refers to not being able to help oneself. I have to empty myself of me to make room for Jesus. The world promotes self-sufficiency or at the present time government sufficiency. In Isaiah 57:15, it says "God dwells with the man whose heart is broken." Dependence upon God starts with the acknowledgement of sin in my life. I have to receive and believe in Jesus Christ (Acts 16:31; Romans 10:9, 10). When this decision is made, the promise of inheriting the kingdom will provide enablement.

Power, energy and strength are found in the centerpiece of God's attributes, "hallowed be thy name" (Matthew 6:9). God has asked me to live in harmony with who he is. This opens up a whole dimension of reverence, respect, awe, appreciation, honor, glory, adoration and worship. To hallow God's name means to hold his matchless being in reverence so that we will believe what he says and will obey him. When I live by faith and bear fruit in my character, I will exalt God's name. When I fear God, I will have the necessary ingredient of life which opens the door to everything good (Psalm 111:10; Proverbs 1:7, 8, 13).

I am learning to be repentive (mournful). Jesus said, "Blessed are they that mourn for they shall be comforted" (Matthew 5:4). Mourning refers to a sincere sorrow for sin. God hates sin and I should also. It grieves him but I like to make excuses for it. Tolerance deception and blindness will create a blockage to growth. Repentance means a change of mind. It is a thorough change in the heart from sin to God. I have to be mournful not only because of the consequences of sin and the baseness of sin but also the divine compassion provided in salvation. I have to "...put to death whatever belongs to my earthly nature" (Colossians 3:5). It says in God's model prayer "thy kingdom come." The source of power is in the fact that God reigns. The worlds attitudes must be replaced with God's. I have to let God remake me and not allow the world to squeeze me in (Romans 12:2). It takes conviction and obedience to pave the way to fulfill God's desires for me (John 14:21). The

Scripture must be the dominant influence on my thoughts, attitudes and actions. I know that it will work (Psalm 119:11). To understand what is right or wrong to do, I have to ask myself, 'is it helpful physically spiritually and mentally?' Does it bring me under its power? Does it hurt others? Does it glorify God? (1 Corinthians 6:12; 8:13; 10:31). I have learned to hate sin and be sensitive to it. I must confess it and accept God's comfort in my repentance.

I am learning to surrender (meek). Jesus said, "Blessed are the meek for they shall inherit the earth." Meekness refers to living for the glory of God. There is no room for self-will. Meekness is not weakness but a display of strength. It is possible through God's grace. I have to learn to accept God's dealings with me without resistance or disputes. No more rebelling or fighting against God. The Holy Spirit makes this possible (Romans 8:26, 27). I have to live life in relationship with his sovereignty (thy kingdom come). I do not have to figure out the plan (thy will be done). If I allow my inner judge of moral issues to be in tune with Jesus

Christ and if I make decisions through a righteous common sense and obey the special assignments given to me, I will be doing everything in his name (thy name). "The kingdom of God is not meat and drink but righteousness, peace and joy in the Holy Ghost" (Romans 14:17).

I am learning to crave (hunger). Jesus said, "Blessed are they that hunger and thirst after righteousness for they shall be filled." He also says, "Give us this day our daily bread." Contentment can only be experienced through craving after righteousness. When I have a craving for something, I cannot leave it alone. It has a driving force behind it. This can be a good thing that takes place or a bad thing. Proof of my spiritual rebirth is found in my desire to pursue God. The inner passion is a blessing. God will provide an intense, sensitive and energetic response to his Word. I am not a victim of worldliness or my own weaknesses. God gives the daily nourishment needed.

I am learning to practice empathy (mercy). In Jesus' own words he says, "Blessed are the merciful for they shall obtain mercy." He also says in his model prayer "forgive us our debts as we forgive our debtors." Mercy is defined as being compassionate. Compassion is having a feeling of deep sympathy. Sympathy is the ability to share the feelings of another and this leads to empathy. Empathy is identifying with an experience of the feeling and thoughts of another. Someone told me that it is like getting in the skin of another. Mercy becomes a part of my life because I have obtained mercy. The Holy Spirit produces mercy. Jesus himself became the ultimate example of this when he cried from the cross, "Father, forgive them for they know not what they do" (Luke 23:34).

When I get in touch with God, I can feel his mercy at work on my behalf. It started when I trusted in him and he gave me a clean heart and peace within. When I receive mercy, I then can share his mercy with others. I pray that I can be sensitive to others that cross my path. I hope I can sense their hopelessness and need.

I am learning to be genuine. In Jesus' own words, he says "Blessed are the pure in heart for they shall see God." He also says in his model prayer "And lead us not into temptation but deliver us." God is doing a work in me. He is conforming me into the image of Christ (Romans 8:29) whose image consists in "righteousness and true holiness" (Ephesians 4:24). Purity of heart is a part of my election and redemption (Ephesians 1:4; Titus 2:14). This is not sinlessness but the truth within (Psalm 51:6). It means a single heart. I am not divided between God and the world. I realize that this calls for radical living. The world praises pride and not humility. The world endorses sin. The world is at war with God. Righteousness will cause persecution. Conflict will take place. Since my life has been transformed by the grace of God, I will see him. Daily faith will bring me into his presence.

I am learning to be in harmony (peacemaker). Jesus said, "Blessed are the peacemakers for they will be called children of God." He also said in his model prayer "For thine is the Kingdom." I have come to the realization that harmony with God will bring peace. With the regeneration power of the gospel in my life, I have experienced peace with God. I am able to be an ambassador of God's message of peace to a troubled world because I daily experience the peace of God in my life.

There have been many times that I have stood between enemies. The Holy Spirit apparently was present to protect me. My attitude of peace caused such a stir and confusion that those enemies did not know what to do. They would lay down their fists and with humility say 'what should we do?' That gave me the opportunity to share the true peacemaker.

I am learning to be victorious in suffering (persecuted). Jesus said, "Blessed are they which are persecuted for righteousness sake." He also said in his model prayer "For thine is the power and the glory forever." The Bible says, "Yea and all that will live godly in Christ Jesus shall suffer persecution" (2 Timothy 3:12). I know that suffering can be experienced through being kept from ones' goal, being tempted through social enterprise, through the presence of the world and can be produced by fellow Christians. Someday

I may experience suffering through physical abuse. I have to learn to practice God's presence all day long. "The Lord is near to all who call on him" (Psalm 145:18).

Jesus never promised ease to those of us he called to follow him. Reliance upon Jesus will cause radical living. Ridicule will most likely pursue us but keep in mind a reward will follow. Jesus lived through persecution, he died through persecution and he rose again after the persecution.

How Do I Handle the Impossible Situations?

In my impossible situation, I sought to glorify God. My second heart attack and open heart surgery placed me into a situation of total dependence upon God. I have had a good relationship with God. I delight in getting acquainted with my heavenly Father though his Son and the Holy Spirit's help. I talk to Jesus like I talk to a friend. He is my best friend. In my pain, my first response was to cry out for his help. This new adventure has been traveled with the Almighty beside me and the people that are close to me. I have discovered that to live in faith, love and hope will bring glory, honor and praise to God.

God has provided faith (Ephesians 2:8, 9). My believing heart has the ability to live by faith

(2 Corinthians 5:7; Galatians 2:20; Hebrews 11). It is nothing that I have done. It is based on the character of the one I believe in (Romans 4:17-21). It is not based upon emotions or circumstances. It is based upon God's attributes. Faith is essentially a decision and is a choice to put the Scripture into practice. Trust is motivated by love for God (Acts 16:31; Romans 4:17-21; Hebrews 11:24-29). The practice of faith made it possible to face the impossible. All I had to do was to mix the Word of God with faith. Having practiced this method of living in little decisions made it possible to handle the big issues. My transformed life has been surrounded with God's promises. God has brought faith into my life. I am learning to rest in an infinite God. He can certainly take care of the body, soul and spirit that he has created.

God has provided love (Genesis 1:27; 2:24; 3:8). In his creation, man was given the ability to love. Love is based in the grace of God. It is a response to his love for me (1 John 4:19). I have discovered that love is an action initiated by a decision (Deuteronomy 7:7; Jeremiah 2:2; 1 Corinthians 13:4-7). Love is a person. It has a person as its object. Love has enabled me to obey the Scripture and it has established my fellowship with God. My decision of faith has put the Word of God into practice with trust. My decision of love has placed God in his rightful place in my life. I entered into this journey with a sovereign God in charge. I was able to have confidence and trust because of who he is. It pleased God to trust him in the impossible. His love was infused in me and brought peace. I knew he had my best interest in mind. He will sustain me and bring power and strength that only he can provide.

God has provided hope. Hope is related to faith and love. This is why the three are often described as united in a single thought or emotion (1 Thessalonians 1:3). Hope is confident expectation in God's person and Word. I have learned to be confident in my trust because of his Word (Psalm 119:43,49,74,81,114,147). I have to choose to believe God (faith), give him his rightful place in my life (love) and apply this to my future (hope). Through my impossible situation, he has enabled me to expect him to work and bless. I believe in God and love him. I accept all that comes into my life as related somehow to his goodness and thank him for it (1 Thessalonians 5:16-18). He has promised to work it all according to good (Romans 8:28, 29).

I learned to handle the impossible through watching God work it out for his glory. I entered into this unexpected attack, uncertain decisions, roller coaster trip, life-functioning machines and open heart surgery with one thought, "Lord, please help me to glorify you through this new experience." He provided faith, love and hope to emerge from my spirit, soul and body. Every hour his grace would appear through my wife, son and daughter, grandkids, extended family, friends, medical staff and the church community.

18

What Do I Do with Doubt?

When doubt challenges me, I must immediately respond. I have to accept the challenge and push forward realizing that God's grace will supply my every need. I cannot just sit. I have to do something. I have learned that doubt is released from my heart when I honestly decide to rest in God's promises. The promises of God are not given to mock me but to give power for daily living. I have to accept the truth that God wants to enable me to live for him. God cannot fail. I have to keep in mind that in my enthusiasm I have to be careful in any misinterpretation of the promises. If I claim the wrong promise, it will not work.

The promises work because of the one who is the source. "The God of peace" (Hebrews 13:20, 21) gives a solid assurance to every promise. The strength of any promise is found in its author. God has given me his Word and he expects me to believe him and to obediently translate this promise on to all of its practical benefits for daily life. He became my enablement. "The God of peace" wants me to be redeemed. As a God of peace, he is for me in every conceivable way. I cannot earn his grace but he is willing to give it. In believing, trust takes place and the blessing of the promise.

The words "brought again from the dead" provides the power. God's provision for me is a person (the Lord Jesus) who took upon himself my penalty and redeemed me by his own sacrifice. The proof that his work was sufficient is in the resurrection. God has met my need for reconciliation, forgiveness, freedom from sin and Satan, wisdom and power to live. The release of doubt is possible through Jesus Christ. I am blessed with a 'great shepherd. I am able to live with confidence because my shepherd is on top of all the issues in life. Security is found in every step of life because of the covenant based upon Christ's blood that was shed on the cross for me. God is equipping me. It is a slow developmental process. God provides the means for me to glorify him. My heavenly Father does the cultivating, my Savior is the mediator and the Holy Spirit gives the moment by moment power.

19

Why Be Depressed?

When depression strikes and the mind needs to become 'sound,' there is guidance available (2 Timothy 1:7; Psalm 32:7, 8). The word 'sound' means disciplined or having self-control. My mind can be guided by supernatural power. "Thou art my hiding place" (v. 7). In my experiences, I have found instruction through the spiritual, psychological and physical. My mind and heart were directed to keep loving Jesus Christ (concerned issue), to keep seeking Jesus Christ (worry issue), to keep abiding in Jesus Christ (anxiety issue) and to keep trusting Jesus Christ (depression issue). It is important to clearly define the conditions of the issues. I am not talking about extreme conditions nor am I giving a diagnosis, but the simple journey that I have taken through my open heart surgery and cancer adjustments.

I must give total love (Keep loving Jesus — Matthew 22:37). This love directs my thoughts. This love is the dynamic of my actions. This love is total commitment. It is not based upon sentiment but a decision. I need to love God with my heart, soul, mind, strength, possessions and service. It involves the will. This love is based upon my relationship with God who provides love through his Son, Jesus, who is my Savior. The infusion of love comes through the Holy Spirit. The Scripture says, "if God were your Father, you would love me . . ." (John 8:42). I have to believe on who Jesus is and act on it in my life through obedience. This love is made possible through how I answer a previous question in Matthew 16:15, "Whom say you that I am?" Making a decision about Jesus Christ is a matter of life and death. I am glad that I am not blind by tradition, position and selfish pride. I love him because he has fulfilled God's grace.

When I am concerned about something and my mind is uneasy about it, I have to focus on my love of Jesus. As I focus on him, he solves the concern. He knows what is best for me. His timing is perfect. The concern is quenched with the Holy Spirit providing a solution. As I keep loving Jesus, love replaces the concern.

If I don't allow love to bring a solution to my uneasy thoughts, my concerns may develop into worry (Keep seeking Jesus — Matthew 6:33). Disturbing thoughts can be changed. I must keep loving Jesus and seek him. I do not have to be confused and worried. I can develop a sound mind and replace the worry through seeking. This takes discipline and dedication. "All these things shall be added unto me if I seek his righteousness." Right thinking takes place as I decide to do what God wants me to do. Worry cannot survive in the atmosphere of tranquility and security. Worry means to divide the mind but peace means to unite the mind. "As he thinketh in his heart, so is he" (Proverbs 23:7). The uneasy and disturbed mind can be controlled. I cannot think fear and act courage. I am what I think. As I seek Jesus and right thinking, my thought process will change.

"Think on things that are true" (Philippians 4:7, 8). Don't think on falsehood. Worries will increase if I think on falsehood. My own heart and mind will condemn me. Think on things that are honest. My thoughts will externalize themselves. Refuse to think about anything that is dishonorable. Think on things that are pure. Impure thoughts will always precede an impure deed. Pure thoughts are incompatible with worry thoughts. Think on things that are lovely. This refers to pleasing thoughts. Embrace them and think on things that are good. I have to get rid of negative thoughts and have to surround myself with optimism, not pessimism. Self-destruction and fear produces thoughts that are sinful. In the strength of God, I can control my thoughts. They can be regulated according to the will of God. Thinking Biblically will replace worry. The Lord is near (Psalm 119:151a; Colossians 1:27). I have to keep seeking Jesus and pursue righteousness (Hebrews 4:15, 16).

Anxiety follows the steps of a negative response to concern and worry. (Keep abiding in Jesus). It constantly is an urgent problem of today. It seems that in this century, we have everything at our fingertips and yet anxiety has become the official emotion of the age. Anxiety is the combination of an inner feeling of uneasiness (negative concern response), disturbing thoughts (negative worry response) and now tensed thoughts (negative anxious response). I realize that there are different levels of anxiety. The 'normal' deep concern — a real threat. The 'chronic' long lasting worry — a habitual worrier. The 'acute' high intensity and overwhelmed — short duration. The 'neurotic' inner conflict, exaggerated feeling — panic. Keep in mind "The Lord shall fight for you and you shall hold your peace" (Exodus 14:14). I have to accept Jesus' strength. When anxiety strikes, I have to be equipped by him. In Hebrews 13:20, 21, I have the promise to be equipped to deal with life's problems. "Make you perfect" emphasizes that I am in a developmental process. God provides the training. He becomes the resource. He will accomplish his will. The next phrase "every good work to do his will" provides the goal. My purpose of being is to glorify God and to please him in everything. He provides the means to accomplish it. The positive response is found in John 15:4, "As the branch cannot bear fruit of itself, except it abide in the vine; so neither can you, except you abide in me."

The word 'abide' occurs ten times in this passage (1-10). Unbroken connection is the key. It is a productive life. "I have spoken these things to you that my joy might be in you" (John 15:11-17). When I am concerned, worried or anxious, I can have deliverance because I have been redeemed through Christ's blood. "Through the blood of the everlasting covenant," I have security. The eternal counsel or God enables me. God has promised to sustain me. There is no fear in love. He cares for me. Anxiety can be released through replacing it with abiding in Jesus Christ.

The doubtful, disturbed, distressed and depressed mind have something in common — deliverance. (Keep trusting Jesus — Proverbs 3:5,6). Nothing is impossible when you put your trust in Jesus. 'Dark days' is a good description of depression. It is full of discouragement, despair, doubt and confusion. Depression is a common but complicated condition. It is hard to describe with accuracy and not easy to treat. Depression is not just being sad. Genetic, biological and environmental factors play into this illness. Attention to the spiritual has to be considered too. Depression is complex because it deals with the inability to function normally and also deals with remaining in touch with reality in others.

I have been encouraged by talking with people experiencing depression at different levels. "Weeping may endure for a night but joy cometh in the morning" (Psalm 30:5). "He healeth the broken hearted" (Psalm 147:3). "Fear not" (Isaiah 41:10). Some people have plunged into depression but eventually come through and experienced a new and lasting joy. "Now may the God of hope fill you with all joy and peace in believing that you may abound in hope by the power of the Holy Spirit" (Romans 15:13). Inaction is common in depressed people. To change feeling, we must change our thinking. I am thankful for intercession that has taken place. When a person is paralyzed with a doubtful, disturbed, distressed and depressed mind, intercession has to take place.

The Spirit of God makes intercession for me. Intercession is made for me not only by God the Son, who sits at the right hand of God the Father, and the Holy Spirit who dwells within me, but also by believers that have become my friends. When the mind is well, release it to God. Dependency is on "the Lord is my shepherd; I shall not want" (Psalm 37:3). "Wait patiently for the Lord . . . he will hear my cry" (Psalm 40:1). "Be pleased, O Lord, to deliver me" (Psalm 40:13). Accept the comfort of the Holy Spirit; he will abide with me forever (John 14:16).

20

What About the Fear of Death?

I can exit from this earth with confidence and with hope because my security is in Jesus. I have many favorite Scriptures but this one may be at the top of the list. "Let not your heart be troubled" (John 14:1). This is the foundational statement of the entire chapter. At death, our hearts can be sometimes troubled, disturbed, emotionally drained, confused, lost, sad and restless. Through Jesus' death, resurrection and ascension we can find rest in knowing the truth. "Ye believe in God, believe also in me" (John 14:1). Believing is the key in having a chariot ride to a new address. It is traveling from earth to heaven. It is an exodus and an arrival. If I believe in Jesus, I have access to God the Father. Keep in mind that death was caused by sin. Death is the end of physical life. Death has been swallowed up in victory. Death is a restful sleep for the body.

"In my father's house are many mansions" (John 14:2). Death is not a hopeless plunge into the vast unknown. It is an adventure into another level of life. "Absent from the body, present with the Lord" (2 Corinthians 4:14-5:3). Jesus said, "I am the way to heaven" (10:9). He said, "I am the embodiment of truth" (8:32). He said, "I am the source of life" (1:4; 3:16). To know Christ is to know the Father. To know the Father brings access to heaven. It all begins with the Holy Spirit urging me to respond to Jesus Christ and my decision to respond opens the door of God's heaven for me.

Jesus said, "I go to prepare a place for you" (John 14:12). Let your hearts be settled and not troubled. The transition and departure removes the tears from troubled hearts (Romans 12:15). It will remove fear from the mind (Hebrews 2:15). It will remove helplessness from the soul (Isaiah 41:10). It will remove hopelessness from the spirit (Psalm 23:4) and remove unhappiness from life (Revelation 14:13). When our soul and spirit is troubled through the death of a loved one, grief is an important and normal response. Whenever a part of life is removed, there is grief. As a follower of Jesus Christ, we take comfort in the certainty of the resurrection. This does not soften the emptiness and pain of being forced to let go of someone we love. Tears, emptiness, loneliness and grief can be understood and strengthened. We know that death is swallowed up in victory (1 Corinthians 15:52-54). We must learn to live and die in the shadow of the Almighty (Psalm 91:1, 2). Our minds have to believe that Jesus cares for those that have fallen asleep. Our spirits have to believe that death is not the end of existence but the entrance into life eternal. As a matter of fact, the believer "shall never die" (Hebrews 2:14, 15). In our reaching inward, outward and upward, the Holy Spirit will give supernatural comfort and peace. These are not glib thoughts. Death is hard.

I believe if we live under the shadow of the Almighty, we will exit from this world with confidence. May I share some testimonies that represent different levels of spirituality and physical experiences? They all seem to sense a "presence" that gave them peace and a restful spirit. These testimonies are from people that have had the shadow of the Almighty in their life. Fear in the mind, helplessness in the soul, hopelessness in the spirit and unhappiness from life have found a release in discovering security in Jesus Christ. In the retirement home after many years of living, a mother would wait for God's call home. "I am ready — my body is weak and my mind is forgetting things I should remember. This is a new experience and I am concerned. I believe in the Bible and I have trusted in Jesus to be the resurrection and the life. I am not worried about death and what will happen five minutes later. God's promises have always been true. The journey to death is scary but I have been assured of his presence. My trials will not be beyond me to handle." I walked into her room after hearing the news of her passing with tears flowing from my eyes. She was curled up like a little baby with a peacefulness that could be seen in her face. She was now face to face with Jesus her Savior. I remember when we were discussing death that we were both reminded that at the moment the angels would come to escort us up to his presence. He would provide strength, confidence and peace. I took her hand and thanked God for his goodness and mercy.

In a hospital room, I found myself responding to a request to visit a relative of a friend. The friend was concerned for the salvation of the sick relative. The man was not doing well and I was told that he was dying. I was the only one in the room and I was his last visitor. I asked the Lord for help. I was reminded that he was in the Lord's hands. I got close to his ear and mentioned his relative's name. I said I was there to introduce him to Jesus Christ. I had just finished sharing the gospel message and he vomited blood all over. The nurse came in and cleaned him up. I was on a special mission. The patient took my hand, his eyes were closed and he whispered into my ear and took his last breath of air. There was no struggle and there seemed to be a release of his soul to the soul maker. I hope so.

In the hospice care center where he was placed to give him as much comfort as possible, an uncle was lying unconscious. His life had hidden secrets that came to the surface during his illness and especially now in his dying. Through spiritual sensitivity and discernment, many of the unexpected issues were discussed with concerned people. I learned that he was a believer in Jesus Christ. With that assurance, I proceeded to pray that he would relax in Jesus. I talked about his escort to heaven. He responded by sitting up, smiling and his heart stopped beating.

In his home, a friend shared his death journey with me. He started with agonizing and excruciating pain that ended in the loss of consciousness. The emergency helpers all arrived to assist. His heart stopped. He was blue one minute and the next he was dead. His trip was brief. It was delightful, pleasant, quiet and peaceful. My friend said the death route was awesome and beyond words to describe. He said he did not want to return but the voyage ended with successful resuscitation. He wished he could have remained on the voyage because he never felt such an awesome experience of serenity. Apparently he had something yet to do. He said these encouraging words, "I know one thing, I will not fear death, when God's timing is right. I will take Jesus' hand again and begin the journey." Let us live life with a Christ-conscious intimacy which will bring us to his presence with peace in death.

21

How Can I Be Secure During Trials?

I have learned that having a life in Christ will bring trials. I face three enemies; the world, the flesh and the devil (Ephesians 2:1-3). 'The world' refers to the system around me that is opposed to God, that caters to "the lust of the flesh and the lust of the eyes and the pride of life" (1 John 2:15-17). 'The flesh' is the old nature that I inherited from Adam, a nature that is opposed to God and can do nothing spiritual to please God. By his death and resurrection, Christ overcame the world (John 16:33; Galatians 6:14) and the flesh (Galatians 2:20; Romans 6:1-6) and the devil (Ephesians 1:19-23). I can be secure during my trials, testing and temptations because victory has already been provided for me.

Victory is achieved when my mind is controlled by the Holy Spirit. My heart is motivated through God's love and Jesus Christ has become the central person in my life. It starts with responding to this command ". . . take captive every thought to the obedience of Christ" (2 Corinthians 10:5). What does it mean to take captive? I have to learn to take charge and place the strongholds, trials and devices into Christ's hands. Confidence can be present in making the right decisions.

'Every thought' refers to all oppositions that need to be placed under the power of God. Confidence can be discovered in action. 'To the obedience' are the key words for success in overcoming. They require repentance, submission and discipline. This is the armor that I have to choose to practice if I am going to have confidence. I must be controlled by truth — Christ is the truth. A clear conscience brings victory. I must be righteous in Christ — Christ is my righteousness. An upright life will allow no accusations from the enemy. I must be committed to the gospel which brings peace — Christ is my peace. Peace with and of God will provide security and strength during the battle. I must be active in relying upon God's promises — Christ is my faith. Satan's fiery darts cannot penetrate me. I must be controlled by God's mind — Christ is my salvation. Satan cannot lead me astray. I must be knowledgeable of his Word — Christ is the Word. The Word will detect Satan's lies and keep me from sin.

Personal Response

Why Should I Glorify God?

In my time of 'trouble' (surgery), I responded to this verse "and call upon me in the day of trouble" (Psalm 50:15). I definitely called on God for help. The verse continued with "I will deliver thee" (hospitalization). God promises to work everything out for my good and his glory certainly became a reality in my life. It ended with "thou shall glorify me" (recovery). I have wanted to glorify him from day one. How this would turn out would be in his hands. I had to let go of myself. He is in charge.

The glory of God refers to his worth (Genesis 31:1), to his power (Genesis 45:13), to his excellence (1 Chronicles 16:10,24,27,35), to his greatness (Deuteronomy 5:24), to his holiness (Isaiah 6:1-3), to his divine manifestation (Hebrews 1:1-3, and to his loving grace (John

1:14). When I personally think of his glory, I think of these words; splendor, superiority, sovereignty, Savior and shepherd. His glory is the total of his essence and attributes. God is glorious because he is God.

I prayed "help me to glorify you through this experience in my life." I had no idea how it would bring honor, praise and glory to himself. It started with my primary focus. He is my refuge (during surgery), strength (during each initial day) and present help (during recovery). This was established through my belief in the Son of God. My salvation in Jesus Christ was secure.

My spiritual transformation is based upon a personal relationship that continues to grow. Negative thoughts will not be found in my mind. I believe in a positive redemption. My counsel will come from the law of God. The Bible has become a dependable source for me. Its claims come from an all-knowing, all-powerful, personal and only existing God. I am convinced through careful research, study experience and inner witness.

The foundation for my coping with the unexpected open heart surgery and cancer is based upon God's promises. I have had to learn to listen to his words and then do them. "Drawing near to him" (James 4:8) has brought a sound, beneficial, righteous, fruitful and pleasant result. As I draw near to him, he will draw near to me. The result will be his presence, love, grace, sovereignty, glory, justice and wisdom. I learned to handle the impossible through watching God work it out for his glory. He provides everything I need at the time I need it, not before or after, but at the moment. Before I entered into this journey, I had the right attitude toward God and life. I believe in God's goodness and I interpret life from his viewpoint.

My days will have gladness and sadness. I experience strength and weakness. I will succeed through victory and defeat. "The Lord is my shepherd, I shall not want" (Psalm 23:1). I have experienced some setbacks. The road is not always upward. It would be nice to say that the journey was pleasant without some doubt.

Human nature would not be natural if that was the story. Circumstances, anxious thoughts, stress and unexpected issues all contribute to the throwing of doubt into the path. I have to do something about this. My weary mind can be changed. God provides the refueling process. I am going to pursue glorifying God and understanding its meaning. Whatever happens, I will obey 1 Corinthians 10:31).

How Can I Live for the Glory of God?

I can live for the glory of God through daily affirming the Scriptures where it says, "I will praise thee, O Lord my God, with all my heart, and I will glorify thy name for evermore" (Psalm 86:12). I am looking for ways to glorify God in my life. I want to live out the faith, love and hope I have experienced. My story has revealed how God used faith (the foundation of my life), love (the motivation behind my life) and the hope (that includes the others together with expectation in my life). The Bible says, "Let your light so shine before men that they may see your good works and glorify your Father which is in heaven" (Matthew 5:16). This refers to actions in my life. Do I display honesty, mercy, righteousness, kindness, gratitude, joy and patience?

The Bible says, "Herein is my Father glorified, that you bear much fruit, so shall you be my disciples" (John 15:8). Bearing fruit is a manifestation of my life in Jesus Christ. I can bear fruit through good works (Matthew 5:16), through purity (1 Corinthians 6:19, 20), through trust (Romans 4:19, 20), through unity (Romans 15:5, 6), through service (1 Peter 4:10, 11), through prayer (John 14:13), through subjection (2 Corinthians 9:12, 13), and through honesty (1 Peter 2:12). My personal response is found in 1 Corinthians 10:31, Whether therefore you eat or drink or whatsoever you do, do all to the glory of God." As I allow the word of Christ to saturate my life, I will glorify God.

24

What Are Some Hindrances to Living for the Glory of God?

I will miss the mark in glorifying God if I fail to understand the greatness of God (Isaiah 40:25, 28). The very nature of God needs to be understood. He is infinite, absolute, unchangeable and perfect in all his ways. All I have to do is ponder on these attributes: his faithfulness (my doubt), his holiness (my sinfulness), his love (my selfishness), his sovereignty (my anxiousness), his truth (my falsehood), his absolute knowledge (my questioning), his powerful nature (my fear), his presence everywhere (my panic) and his lordship (my disobedience).

He is absolutely in control over all of his creation. He rules over the affairs of men and does whatever he chooses (Job 23:13). He can do whatever he wants to do simply because he owns everything (Psalm 24:1). All the details of my life will not escape him and whatever purpose he has for me, he will achieve. I will miss the mark in glorifying God if I fail to understand the goodness of God (Exodus 34:6). I have to learn to evaluate the person and work of God from God's perspective, not from my emotion and circumstances.

His goodness is found in his creation. If I understand that I was formed by and for him my life would become revolutionary. I was made to glorify him. I have been created by God, that determines my worth. I have been redeemed by God. That determines my peace. I have been created by God for himself. That determines my fulfillment. No longer is there confusion, failure, weakness and instability. His goodness has taken over.

God's goodness can be defined through reading Psalm 119:68, "Thou art good and doest good." He is good by his nature and by what he does. Every good thing bestowed and every perfect gift is from above, coming down from the

Father of lights. God only produces that which is good. Keep in mind that God is sovereign. He allows things for reasons we do not always understand. There is no sin or defect in him. My challenge is to respond and rely upon his words, "No good thing does he withhold from those who walk uprightly" (Psalm 84:11). God can change negatives into positives. He causes all things to work together. When I reflect on God's goodness, my prayer is "Oh give thanks to the Lord for he is good; for his lovingkindness is everlasting" (Psalm 107:1, 2).

I will miss the mark in glorifying God if I fail to understand the graciousness of God. I will never forget a little chorus I sang as a child. It has three main emphases. The chorus became my theme song. It was based upon the New Testament book of Ephesians. "His very own, wonderful grace to his word is made know, chosen by the Father, purchased by the Son, sealed by the Spirit, I'm his very own" (Sidney E. Cox). God's grace is not deserved. It cannot be earned and be abused. Grace is God's unmerited favor. I would like to begin each day with "grace be to you" and end with "to the praise of the glory of his grace" (1:2, 6). Grace is the divine and free favor of God. It comes with tranquility and is a result of the reconciliation that has taken place between God and man based on faith in the union with the Lord Jesus Christ. The source of spiritual blessings comes from a heavenly Father and Jesus Christ. The blessings are unmerited. They are a product of the Holy Spirit. I am able to be blessed because I am 'in Christ.' This is the key. Nothing is too good or too great for God to bestow upon me. Grace goes before me because God has chosen. Jesus is my mediator (1 Timothy 2:5). Grace finds its foundation in the will of God. God's choice was eternal and his plan is timeless. I either receive or reject God's provision in Christ. Grace goes before me and enables me (Romans 8:29). Holiness is the positive side of a Christ like life (Hebrews 12:14). God expects me to live by his standards. Grace goes before me and provides for my adoption. I have been placed into his family. I am "his very own according to the good pleasure of his will" (v.5). The purpose of God's grace is to receive glory. He receives glory as I praise him in my vital relationship with his Son. God is totally self-sufficient. I cannot demand anything nor do I deserve anything. Living in his grace is my joy (Galatians 2:20).

What Priorities Should I Pursue to Glorify God?

I have to shine brightly to reveal good works to glorify God (Matthew 5:13-16). Because I am in Christ and he is in me, I can live out his beatitudes that will glorify him through my attitude and actions. I can discern my true condition before God. It is the spiritual awareness of the distance between infinity and finiteness. It is the repentant cry of my heart as I stand in the shadow of Calvary and look up into the loving face of the one who suffered in my place. It is serving in humility with meekness, hunger, mercy and righteousness.

I have to pray with boldness to glorify God. "And whatsoever you shall ask in my name, that will I do that the Father may be glorified in the Son" (John 14:13). Jesus wants to be involved with my daily life of prayer. To pray in his name means that I am praying in his will. I am learning to saturate my mind with his. It takes discipline, devotion and dedication. What a privilege it is to talk to God through his Son and the guidance of the Holy Spirit. Daily breathing should become a part of my breathing in his word and intimate communication with him.

I have to understand my identification with Christ to glorify God (Romans 6:4). I have died in Christ and I have been raised in his resurrection. This simply means that I may not allow any sin in my life and I must be characterized by all forms of virtue. Living in harmony with my union in Christ must be demonstrated.

I have to mix his word with faith to glorify God (Hebrews 4:1-3). I have to be more than willing to do God's will. I have to do it. I have to aggressively mix the Word of God with faith. I have to practice trusting God. This involves knowledge and application of his word, "Be ye doers of the word and not hearers only" (James 1:22-24). I must learn the word, put it into practice by faith and do it all for the glory of God.

I have to please the Lord with thanksgiving to glorify him. Thanksgiving should be spontaneous. It should be a daily activity in my life (John 6:11; 11:41). I am thankful to God for himself and for his greatness, goodness and graciousness. As I seek to understand his infinity, his attributes, his work and grace, I come before him in gratitude. Without his mercy, I would be lost. I am thankful for his counsel and how it endures generation after generation.

Personal Response

Sources

Barnes, Albert — Matthew and Mark — Baker Book House 1956

Barnes, Albert — Luke and John — Baker Book House

Berry, George R — The Interlinear — Greek English New Testament, Zondervan Publishing House

Halley, Henry — Bible Handbook — Chicago, Illinois 1927

Martin, Alfred — John-Life Through Believing, Moody Press 1959

Tenney, Merrill C. — John, the Gospel of Belief, Wm Eerdman's Publishing Company 1953

Unger and Merrill F — Unger's Bible Dictionary, Moody Press 1957

Wuest, Kenneth S — The Gospels, Wm Eerdman's Publishing Company 1955

Falwell, Jerry — Liberty Bible Commentary, The Old-Time Gospel Hour 1983

Wiersbee, Warren — Be Compassionate, Chariot Victor 1988

Barclay, William — The Gospel of Luke, Westminster Press 1956

Boice, James Montgomery — Foundations of the Christian Faith, Intervarsity Press 1986

Evans, Tony — Our God is Awesome, Moody Press 1994

Geisler, Norman — Unshakable Foundations, Bethany House 2001

Matthew, Victor — Daily Affirmation of Faith, Notes 1980

Unknown, From The Heart — The Life Model 2010

Graham, Billy — Nearing Home, Thomas Nelson 2011

Stowell, Joseph M. — Eternity, Moody Press 1995

Jeremiah, David — When Your World Falls Apart, Thomas Nelson 2000

DeHaan, M.R — Hebrews, Zondervan Publishing House 1959

MacArthur, John — The MacArthur New Testament Commentary Hebrews, Moody Bible Institute 1983

All Scripture quotations are taken from the King James Version of the Bible. Thomas Nelson Incorporated, 1976

Acknowledgements

I appreciate all the people that God has used to influence me. Many of these thoughts have come to my memory over the past seventy-five years through sermon notes, lectures, conversations, meditations and reading. I have not knowingly withheld any significant reference from others in my devotional. To the best of my knowledge, all statements and information are true and correct and given credit. Everyone I have come in contact with should be given credit. The devotional is a constant source of strength, support and security for me and I hope for you.

www.ingramcontent.com/pod-product-compliance
Lightning Source LLC
Chambersburg PA
CBHW070104080526
44586CB00013B/1187